A Trade School for Christian Living
How Churches Can Teach the Skills of Following Jesus

By Rev. Brian and Rev. Micaiah Tanck

2025

OptIN Publishing

www.OptINts.com
OptIN Trade School

Copyright © 2025 OptIN Publishing

All rights reserved. No part of this book may be reproduced or transmitted in any form or by any means, electronic or mechanical, including photocopying, recording, or by any information storage or retrieval system.

The publisher of this book is: OptIN Publishing.

This edition (First Edition) was published for Brian and Micaiah Tanck, and the publisher is responsible for this edition's distribution.

For information about permission to reproduce this edition of the book contact:

OptIN Publishing
Scottsboro Cumberland Presbyterian Church
315 S. Kyle Street
Scottsboro, AL 35768

OptIN Trade School
Website: www.optints.com

The authors, Brian and Micaiah Tanck retain all publishing and distribution rights and permissions. OptIN Publishing is associated with the Scottsboro Cumberland Presbyterian Church.

Brian and Micaiah Tanck:
Brian.Tanck@gmail.com, Micaiah.Thomas@gmail.com
Printed and digital versions are by Amazon. For more information about materials and resources from OptIN, The Trade School for Christian formation, see their website OptIN Trade School (ts) at www.optinTS.com

ISBN #: 978-1-960958-20-4

Dedication

To Scottsboro Cumberland Presbyterian Church that had the patience, courage, and fidelity to walk with us through the doors God has opened.

To the family and friends who encouraged us along the way, especially Lynn who wrote many first drafts.

To Sofia, who helped us understand what church could do.

And to Micaiah, who has always believed in this work enough to take the risk of launching it into the world.

Table of Contents

OptIN 7

Chapter 1 – A Tale of Two Princetons 9
The Esteemed Princeton and the Under-Valued "Stick Town" ... 9
Called to Stick Town 11
Our Church, Our Love 13
Realizing The Need for Change 14

Chapter 2 – The Birth of OptIN 17
Our Story 17
Love for The Theoretical 20
Challenges in Ministry and Our Questions 21
A New Idea - OptIN 24

Chapter 3 – The Core Units 29
Diverse Christian Practices 29
Starting With the Basics 31
Building Faithful Stories 32
Goal of OptIN Story Unit: 35
Practicing Prayer 38
Goal of OptIN Prayer Unit: 40
Rehearsing Worship 44
Goal of OptIN Worship Unit: 48

Chapter 4 – OptIN Methodology 52
Where does Theology fit in? 53
Other Units 54
OptIN Kids 54
A Birthright That's Been Ignored 55

Chapter 5: Trade School Methods and Practices ... 59
Introduction to The Trade School 59

A Willing Heart and Unskilled Hands 62
Apocalyptic Unmasking.. 64
Vocational Pedagogy 66
Christian Practices Suffer from the Fall..................................... 69
The Trade School Pyramid 73

Chapter 6: What We Learned about Learning 75
The Theory of Change.. 75
A Sequence of Skills: Simple to Complex 81
Using the Right Tools 83
Specific Objectives and Concrete Standards............................. 84
Keep It Engaging 85

Chapter 9 – The Fruit of Spiritual Practices 107
Freedom to Practice - Grace 107
The Fruit of Spiritual Practices 110
Testimonials... 111
The Limits of OptIN 121

Chapter 10: Conclusion.. 122

Bibliography 126

OptIN

OptIN is the Trade School for Christian Formation.

A trade school exists to help people develop real skills and become familiar with the tools of a craft—carpentry, plumbing, computer programming, or auto repair. Students begin with simple projects, like building a birdhouse, and move toward complex ones, like constructing a table or a house. The process is hands-on, cumulative, and transformative.

OptIN applies this same approach to Christian life. Faith is not mastered by listening alone but by doing—by practicing, failing, reflecting, and trying again. OptIN helps people develop faith skills through structured, progressive practice. Every tool and exercise is designed for concrete outcomes that strengthen the habits of following Jesus.

Before any skill can be learned, there's a first step: you have to opt in. No one becomes a carpenter—or a disciple—by accident. Trade school is voluntary, not mandatory. It happens in a shop, not a classroom. OptIN invites people to show up and participate in the work of formation together. Rooted in the life and teaching of Jesus—who calls us to "be doers of the word, and not hearers only"—OptIN forms people through action, reflection, and shared life.

This book explains where OptIN came from, how it equips congregations to participate more fully in the life of the church and the personal practices of faith, and why we believe this sort of experimentation is necessary, not optional, for the church today. It introduces the method, shares outcomes we've seen in real communities, and presents the tools we've created for those ready to OptIN. You'll also find stories and reflections from pastors, parents, and participants who have put these practices into motion.

OptIN has been made possible by funding through the Lilly Endowment's Thriving Congregations Initiative. The aim of the national initiative is to strengthen Christian congregations so they can help people deepen their relationships with God, build strong relationships with each other, and contribute to the flourishing of local communities and the world.

Lilly Endowment has made 219 grants with this initiative. The grants will support organizations as they work directly with congregations and help them gain clarity about their values and missions, explore and understand better the communities in which they serve, and draw upon their theological traditions as they adapt ministries to meet changing needs.

Reverends Brian and Micaiah Tanck are pastors of the Cumberland Presbyterian Church in Scottsboro, Alabama, and co-founders of OptIN: The Trade School for Christian Formation.

Chapter 1 – A Tale of Two Princetons

This project exists because of our (Micaiah and Brian) growing love for the church. As with any love, it took root in particularity. This discipleship initiative grew from our love for Scottsboro Cumberland Presbyterian (CP) Church. Scottsboro is nestled in the mountains and lakes of North Alabama, and our church is "That red brick church up on the hill." The center of our life together is a traditional sanctuary with exposed wooden beams, a vaulted ceiling, pews facing split pulpits, and a bronze cross that refuses to stay polished of fingerprints.

The building has come to feel like home for us. Not because of the hours we've spent there over the last ten years. But, because of the people we share that space with. This church took a chance on two just-married, not-yet-ordained, newly-graduated pastors.

One of our first weeks in Scottsboro, a group from the congregation harangued us after worship. They knew we had recently graduated from Princeton Theological Seminary in New Jersey. "This will help you feel at home," they said as we wedged into the third row of a Honda Pilot and took off headed… somewhere.

The Esteemed Princeton and the Under-Valued "Stick Town"

Princeton Seminary is a beautiful campus located a block away from Princeton University. At the University, we had access to a library advertised as second only to the Vatican's library in Vatican City. We walked on cobblestone walkways and passed the bench where Einstein supposedly sat and reflected. A plaque outside our dining hall honored literal martyrs who had graduated from Princeton Seminary before carrying the gospel into hostile corners of the world. The place carried an implicit challenge; "What are you doing to belong here?" Imposter syndrome was endemic. At the same time, you must be worth something to be at Princeton, right?

Ten minutes after pulling out of the church parking lot, after a rural highway turned into a seemingly identical rural highway, we pulled into a cluster of buildings and empty streets. One of our hosts turned with a huge grin. "We're here!"

"Here" had no cell-signal. No traffic. No sidewalks, much less cobblestone walkways. No library, much less one to rival the Vatican. "Here" was Princeton, Alabama. Ten minutes from our new home in Scottsboro, Princeton had a population of 200. The area had a density of 10 people per square mile. We understand why people look at places like Scottsboro and Princeton, Alabama, and all they see is a "stick town." Connection to places like Princeton Seminary validates worth and work. Our new church felt like they were taking a chance on two just-married, not-yet-ordained, newly graduated pastors. When they offered us a contract, we had to ask for a moving allowance to afford the U-Haul to drive ourselves down. We knew they felt like they were taking a chance on us.

Brian and Micaiah, at the (former) grocery store in Princeton, Alabama

But standing there in Princeton, Alabama, it felt like they weren't the only ones taking a chance.

Before moving to New Jersey, Brian lived in the suburbs of Chicago. The first time he said "Y'all" in a children's message with that "Yankee accent," the congregation applauded. Micaiah was raised on the mission field in Colombia, South America until she moved with her family to Birmingham, AL. She had always lived in urban centers.

Now here we were. In Stick Town.

Which is how scripture helped us find our bearings in the backwoods of Alabama. In John's gospel, after Philip is called to follow Jesus, he runs off to tell Nathaneal. Philips says, "Come on, we've found the one of whom Moses in the law and the prophets was writing. It's Jesus of Nazareth." And Nathanael replies, "Nazareth? Can anything good come from Nazareth?" Because Nazareth was on the far side of nowhere. You didn't think about Nazareth unless you lived in Nazareth. It wasn't evil. It wasn't bad. It was country. The likely root for the name "Nazareth" is the Hebrew word for a branch or a stick. As in Isaiah 11:1, "From the stump of Jesse a branch will sprout." A branch. A shoot. A stick.

Nazareth was literally "Stick town." Standing beneath the decrepit sign of that abandoned grocer in Princeton, AL, "Stick Town" felt exactly right.

We started our ministry at Scottsboro CP Church on July 1, 2015. When Micaiah preached the first Sunday at Scottsboro, she opened with the line, "I know, I know. But I promise, I'm older than I look." Something magical happens when you speak the truth. Micaiah is 5 foot, 2 1/2 inches (she insists on the ½) tall. She looks younger than her years. Preaching honestly isn't just about convicting sinners. That first Sunday, it was about honestly naming that this church in the heart of the Baptist Bible Belt had hired a female senior pastor who looked like she was in high school. That's not hyperbole. The next week we went to introduce ourselves as a resource to the high school principal. Instead of escorting us back to meet the principal, the secretary tried to enroll us as new students.

It wasn't the start we had been hoping for.

But we were convinced that it was God that had called us to pack up everything we owned in a U-Haul and move from New Jersey to rural Alabama. We were convinced that God had a plan for us here. So Micaiah stood in the pulpit and spoke truth. The truth that mattered right then was that we looked young and inexperienced because we were, but we were called and willing to serve this church.

Called to Stick Town

Weeks before moving to "Stick Town," we had graduated from Princeton Seminary, and days later were married at Princeton Seminary's chapel. At Princeton, we had each received an M.Div. and an M.A., my second degree being in Youth Ministry and Micaiah's in Spiritual Formation and Mission. Both of us had spent most of our seminary career serving in the local church. The purpose of our education was to live in service of the church. For us, there was something profound in how God was calling us, not just to each other, but to a shared mission for God's Kingdom.

We were gifted with a wedding that was more than just a commitment to each other. The service was a recognition that God had called us to each other for shared service to God's church. Serving together has been one of the great joys of our lives. When God called us together, we imagine it was part of the plan to put our different personalities and styles and preferences into relatively constant creative tension.

This introduction could have been titled, "In defense of Stick Towns." Not to downplay the importance of formalized training or rigorous instruction for church leadership. The church needs properly equipped ministers as much as ever. Our time at Princeton was marked by citations of Eugene Peterson's call to a long obedience in one direction.[1] It was part of a larger attempt to reclaim the necessarily relational character of ministry from the generalities and vagaries of programmatic church culture. Friends and peers regularly admired his call to a long and faithful tenure at one congregation. To know your people. As a pair of contrarians, we can admit it was hard for us to read Peterson until we left seminary. And we can admit we were wrong.

Our initial plan had been to stay in Scottsboro for between 3-5 years, the average tenure of a first call. But over the last 10 years, we have come to love this church. We have been blessed with friends and mentors and co-workers in Christ. It is hard to name exactly when that happened. At some point, it stopped being a job the way it was when we started. It is a family. As with any family, we rely on each other. When life has thrown us sideways, humbled us, and brought us low, this church has been there. As we have married and buried and preached and laughed, our church has come to trust us. Within this church family, we have a particular role. Namely, to make disciples, teaching them to obey all that God has commanded us.

But along the way, we found the call to 'make disciples' more difficult than we had anticipated.

Kenda Dean has borrowed a line to describe invention in the church: "Love makes you an inventor."[2]

And love only grows in particularity. When Jesus calls us to love our neighbor, the example he immediately gives is a story of three different people encountering a man in their path. He is a particular man, with a particular set of problems, and a particular set of alienating attributes. It is not a question of whether they love "humanity" in general. It is undeniably easier to love humanity in general. The question framed by

---

[1] Peterson 2019, The book's title is, "*A Long Obedience in The Same Direction*"
[2] Kenda Creasy Dean, 2016.

this parable is whether these three men can love this particular man. Love is always of the particular.

Our Church, Our Love

When we first started as pastors of SCPC, we discovered that our church was full of earnest and honest Christians. Folks who were there every time the doors were opened. Families who dragged their kids to everything even if the kid only had one shoe on. As we shared life with them, and walked with them through their joys and their tragedies, we began to notice something.

Church wasn't working for them the way we thought it should. They should be experiencing more fruit in their lives.

We preached the gospel. People professed their faith. People experienced belonging and community within our walls. Our attendance increased, and decreased, and increased again. It would have been easy to hide behind different metrics of success. Except that we had come to love these people and this church. And we weren't convinced that church was working.

If you take married co-pastors with some workaholic tendencies and set them loose in a town where everyone they know goes to the church, they will spend a lot of time focused on ministry. And we did. We talked ourselves in circles about services and Christian Education and retreats, about starting a youth group, then a children's ministry, then canceling it. About creative worship experiences that could help people have a fresh encounter of our incredible God. With a trusting Session (church board) behind us, we found ourselves buying confetti cannons to put outside the sanctuary for an Easter surprise and a couple thousand paper cranes to hang from the ceiling for Pentecost.

To embody the death-to-life our church (like so many churches) felt coming out of COVID, we used rolls of aluminum foil to completely black-out all the windows in our sanctuary. The room was pitch-black, except for lamps held by children. Then we ripped down the foil like the Spirit ripped open Jesus' grave.

We treasure those moments. They were faithful and powerful; we hope they helped bring the gospel alive. But was worship changing participants' hearts and minds? Was church affecting their lives the way Jesus and the Spirit, the Bible and church history suggest it can?

Church wasn't working the way we thought it should.

OptIN is the story of different experiments that we've tried to make church work again for this congregation we love. We have tried plenty of things that have failed. One important lesson we have learned is that churches worshipping a God who was resurrected cannot be afraid of failure. Faithful failure is good soil.

Along the way, we've found some success. Because this success is God's and not ours, we think it is our responsibility to share it. More foundationally, we want to further an ongoing conversation around Christian practices and spiritual disciplines in the contemporary.

Which brings us back to a tale of two Princetons.

Realizing The Need for Change

It was through coming to love Scottsboro CP Church that we began to recognize that something wasn't working. It was in this particular church that we began to recognize deficits in standard approaches to Christian formation. How is it that someone can go to church all their life, even for generations, and earnestly profess a faith in Jesus, but find sharing their faith with others impossible? How can people be highly committed, attend every church event, engage in worship, but describe their personal prayer life as insufficient?

The Christian life is not a theory. The Christian life is not a Bible Study. This should be obvious for a people who say God came to earth *in the flesh,* and so believe that the truth is not a book or an idea. The truth is a person. It is Jesus. To believe in Jesus is not to have an idea. To believe in Jesus is to share in his life. Which means the faith inescapably consists of things *we do.* Prayer and worship, testimony and service are all activities. So, we began to move Christian formation out of the classroom and into the workshop. We began experimenting with practices, activities, and skill development as an essential part of Christian discipleship. Experimenting with our congregation, we began to develop an approach we called OptIN, which later became the Trade School for Christian Formation.

Carpentry is a trade. No carpenter learns to build furniture merely by sitting in a classroom, listening to a lecturing professor. They develop skills in a workshop, using tools along the way, with a community of mentors and peers to teach and guide. A carpenter starts by first building a birdhouse, a simple project to begin developing the skills of carpentry. This sets them up to build a table, and then a chair.

What are the Christian "birdhouses" people need to follow Jesus? What are the skills we need to build those "birdhouses?"

Craig Dykstra, vice-president of religion at the Lilly Foundation, states Christian "Practices are those cooperative human activities through which we, as individuals and as communities, grow and develop in moral character and substance".[3] He explains that these practices are the result of the Holy Spirit living in us. They are the power of God in us molding us to do as God does.[4] The more virtuous we are, the more spiritual we are, the healthier our community. The church, our church, is a community. If we can do a better job learning skills of the Christian faith, our church community is all the stronger. The church, generally, does a great job with teaching thoughts and beliefs. Even the design of our buildings demonstrates the importance of knowing beliefs. We have a large meeting hall to sit in and listen and learn (sanctuary), and we have classrooms for smaller breakout groups to listen and learn. But we don't have many workshops in our churches.

OptIN is a workshop, a place to build the habits, skills, and routines needed for Christian flourishing. OptIN lives in the space of practices.

In Matthew 7, Jesus says:

> "Everyone who hears these words of mine and *puts them into practice* will be like a wise man who built his house on the rock. And the rain fell, and the floods came, and the winds blew and beat on that house, but it did not fall, because it had been founded on the rock. And everyone who hears these words of mine and *does not put them into practice* will be like a foolish man who built his house on the sand. And the rain fell, and the floods came, and the winds blew and beat against that house, and it fell, and great was the fall of it." (Matthew 7: 24-27)

---

[3] Dykstra 2005, p. 69

[4] Ibid. p. 66

According to Jesus, it is essential that we ***practice*** following Jesus. Our hope is that OptIN would be a method that churches can apply to their existing structures, so that congregants can put Jesus' words into practice. We want to help men and women build houses on rock, so that when the storms come, they will not fall.

Too many churches today spend most of their time feeling guilty. Guilty for being too small. Guilty for being too old. Conversations about churches thriving are dominated by megachurches: their techniques and their leaders. *What good can come from a little church, where these same people worship week after week?*

When Jesus called Nathanael to follow him, Nathanael asks a simple question, "Can anything good come out of Nazareth?" You see, Nazareth was Nathanael's Stick Town.

When we started talking about OptIN, we got questions like Nathanael's. Just two pastors of a "small" church. "How cute." "How quaint." *What good could possibly come from a place like Scottsboro?!*

Nathanael didn't understand—it wasn't about Nazareth. It was about Jesus. What has happened in our church in Scottsboro, in our Stick Town, hasn't been about us. We have been humbled by the ways God has led us, together, into a lived way of life built on the foundation of Jesus Christ. We have grown to love our Stick Town where something good can come from a group of faithful men and women who intentionally put God's Word into practice.

Chapter 2 – The Birth of OptIN

Try something. Fail. And then try again.

That has been a guiding principle in our ministry. As pastors, we have drawn from our past experiences, our education, and our own ministry failures in leading the church. Our story explains how our backgrounds and challenges along the way, have set us up to learn new things.

Our Story

God has a way of preparing people for work they don't yet know they'll do. Looking back, the skills and experiences that would eventually shape OptIN were being formed long before either Brian or Micaiah knew they would need them.

Brian grew up curious, wanting to understand how things worked. The cars he drew as a child had all the issues with proportion and shape as other cars. But they also had brake lines so the car could stop. His interest in other people kept him in trouble through his early years of school. Teachers would comment, "He's doing ok in class, but Brian would be doing better if he would sit down and listen."

While Brian grew up attending church, sitting in a pew between his parents and grandparents, it wasn't a source of curiosity until high school. It was a fact. Church was a place you went to do church things. God was an important person to be aware of—like the president, or the principal. Until Knox Presbyterian became a foundation for his faith.

Brian fell in love with church before he fell in love with Jesus. At Knox Pres, he found himself part of a community oriented toward abundant life. A group of friends gave an embodied experience of the fellowship of believers. A youth leader pushed him to think deeper, and to live out his faith with greater integrity. Pastoral leaders made space for him to explore his call and gifts.

The belonging and life Brian found in that youth group centered youth ministry for his church work. While only an average student, his time at Calvin College taught him that there were different ways to think. Double majoring in Philosophy and English exposed him to literary criticism, textual analysis, continental and analytic philosophy, all within the constraints of rigorous theological commitments.

After a year of working in a warehouse and interning at his home church, a clarified call to youth ministry led Brian to Princeton Seminary.

Micaiah grew up on the mission field of Colombia, South America. The mission field tends to evoke images of being raised in the jungle, but she wasn't. She was raised in urban cities in Colombia. She is 5th generation Cumberland Presbyterian minister. Her first love, she says, was the Ballet. At the age of 8, she proudly proclaimed to her parents that she was going to be a ballerina. Professionally. So when the family moved to the USA a year later, the first thing Micaiah participated in was a ballet class.

She was a 4th grader, which is far too late to start ballet and be taken seriously. Serious dancers begin at the age of three. But that was no deterrent for her; she loved the art form and the athleticism. She loved communicating through movement, instead of words. And she was determined to be good. Two years into her ballet lessons, she was invited into the advanced track for ballet. That track eventually led her to be a part of the ballet company, "Ballet Exaltation," by the time she was in high school. She went to school, excelled in academics, and danced almost 30 hours/week all through high school.

Her particular ballet company was a part of a Christian Ballet School. It was there that Micaiah learned the power of spiritually engaging God through movement, through the body. Those years of dance "for the glory of God" trained her to appreciate spirituality as more than just talking to God.

While her dream was to pursue a career in ballet, God had other plans. By the time she finished her senior year in high school, she felt less certain about joining a ballet company and more certain about attending college for a degree that would lead her into ministry. She hung up her ballet slippers, and went to school at the University of Alabama. At Alabama, she quickly learned that a touchdown was worth 6 points, not 7, and that Saturdays were a day to wear crimson and white.

It was at the University of Alabama that Micaiah felt deeply called to ordained ministry. Because 'action' is Micaiah's modus operandi, a few months later she found herself pastoring a small church of 30 people in Hueytown, AL.

Kay Cummins, a force in her own right, served as a lay leader of that church, and they needed a pastor. Kay invited Micaiah to preach one Sunday morning (just to fill in). Micaiah agreed. Monday morning after Micaiah preached, Kay gave Micaiah a call. She said, "As you know, we don't have a pastor right now, and we really need some leadership. Would you consider working, functionally, as our pastor during this time? We can pay you $100/week." Micaiah made every excuse she could think of: "I am a college student." "I've never done this before." "I'm only 19 years old." "I live 45 minutes away."

But she couldn't say, "No." She thrives on a challenge, so as a sophomore in college, she was preaching every week, and leading a church through grief and death, through joys and growth. This church in Hueytown helped Micaiah grow, they gave her room to try stuff and fail. Micaiah received a degree in college, but more importantly, she was given a place to practice all the ins and outs of ministry.

After graduation, she left Hueytown for Princeton Seminary, where Micaiah and Brian would finally meet.

Looking back, God was preparing both of them with exactly what OptIN would need. Micaiah was formed by all that is tangible. Her spiritual formation is linked to the movement of the body. It is understood through lived ministry practice. Her past drew her into spiritual formation: a set of practices you do over and over so that you can be drawn into the presence of God. Brian's curiosity about how things work, combined with his philosophical training, would prove helpful for analyzing why traditional approaches weren't producing the fruit churches hoped for and designing systems to respond.

At their wedding, Brian and Micaiah were commissioned into ministry together. Little did they know that this commissioning would prove so fruitful—or that God was already weaving together the skills and perspectives that would eventually become OptIN.

Love for The Theoretical

When we were in seminary, our vision of ministry was shaped by abstracted, large-scale problems. By its nature, a seminary equips students to serve the church in general. Conversations were about problems facing "the church."

We did not become pastors of "The Church." We became pastors of *a* church. We were no longer in a seminary discussion group, talking about "them" and "us." Serving in a particular church, "them" and "us" had become *us*. We were now part of the community, and wanted to be a benefit to those around us. The connection to a specific church demanded our abstracted and generalized understandings be contextualized.

During seminary, we dove into church issues like Moral Therapeutic Deism and declining church attendance. We analyzed various theologians and proposed solutions within our academic bubble, enriched by historical locations. We engaged in typical seminary activities of discussion, study, and writing, mirroring the church's actions.

If you notice your church, as most churches, we discuss, study, sometimes argue, in a classroom or large meeting space. Those conversations in seminary and church are interesting and informative. They certainly can get everyone engaged, at times, even mad. But does learning new ideas take us far enough in our faith journey? Do those ideas change us for the better, or help our church flourish?

Dykstra observed a short-coming of theological training. He said, "When practice means the application of theory to contemporary procedure, then biblical studies, history, systematic theology, philosophy, and ethics all become theoretical disciplines in which practice has no intrinsic place".[5] His point is Christian practice is often associated with learning Christian theory, not hands-on-practices.

The price paid is there is little Christian practice going on in the Church. We substitute learning ideas for learning how to do Christian disciplines. That was not only our seminary background, but it was also a big part of our church background. Amos Yong, professor and dean of Fuller

---

[5] Murphy, Et. al. 2003, p. 163

Theological Seminary, explains that theory and practice are both needed. Practice provides real-life experiences that fuel theory. And theory provides a place for conversations where life and witness are connected to critical thought.[6] Theory that has little or no input from practice, that is, real life experiences, is an empty theory.

We like the story that is purportedly told by Soren Kierkegaard about "the ducks." The ducks waddle to church every Sunday and learn about flying. They sing songs about flying and hear great inspirational messages about flying. Then they receive a benediction to fly well throughout the week and **they all waddle home.**

What if flying is not an abstract idea open for discussion and debate, but a skill development problem? What if the problem with the flightless ducks is not "knowing" the techniques of flying but practicing the skills to "fly"? How many of our churches are full of ducks who learn *about* flying, but only ever *waddle*.

In seminary, there is a preference for the abstract and theoretical. Because seminaries train pastors, this preference trails them into the church. Spend enough years writing papers and analyzing arguments, and the solution to every problem starts to look like writing a paper or analyzing an argument. Less visible, some of this preference for the abstract is rooted in the contemporary church's desire to scale—we want ministries that can apply equally to any child of a particular age, a sermon that can be preached to any generic group of Christians living today. If you're going to buy a curriculum, it will not have been written for your church and its particular people.

Against this preference for the abstract and theoretical, a less common response to the church's challenges is experimentation. But, discipleship should be more than presenting and defending ideas about God's Kingdom. It should be about more than being generically faithful. Because there are no churches in general, or Christians in general. Only particular people, trying to follow our particular God, in the midst of their particular lives.

Challenges in Ministry and Our Questions

---

[6] Yong 2020, p. 36 of 176, Kindle

Early in our ministry at Scottsboro, we had an encounter with a man at our church. He is one of those quiet people, a pillar on which churches are often built. He has had trials in his life, but he has persevered with incredible faithfulness.

The day he met with us was a surprise. We found ourselves sitting together at the church one morning as he expressed his broken heart. Through tears and frustration, he said, "Where is the joy? I don't know what I'm doing wrong, but I don't know how much harder I can try. Why can't I find any joy?"

It would have been easy to theorize why a person of such deep devotion would feel this way. But this wasn't a theoretical problem. It was personal. This wasn't a person. It was one of our people.

Dallas Willard says, "For serious churchgoing Christians, the hindrance to true spiritual growth is not unwillingness".[7] Our friend was a representation of that truth. He was willing, but wasn't experiencing the fruit of spiritual growth. What were we supposed to do?

Should we tell him that he was entering God's presence wrong by faithfully attending *every* Sunday? Should we tell him to do less? To be less willing? Tell him that the Spirit just didn't want him to experience joy in his life? Should we lower his expectations?

Being trained in thoughts and ideas and arguments, it is our habit to address the church's problems with better thoughts and ideas and arguments. But this member of our congregation didn't need better thoughts and ideas. He already agreed with our argument. Despite his fidelity to the church, and despite the fact that our church is orthodox in teaching and practice, he still wasn't receiving what he needed to be fulfilled in his relationship with God.

This encounter pushed us, as pastors, to consider what else we should be doing to form disciples.

We are fortunate to have a congregation with young families, which means we engage a lot of parents of school-aged children. There was a pattern we began to recognize: mothers brought their children to worship, but fathers were not always there. It'd be easy to condemn these

---

[7] Willard 2014, p 18 of 277, Kindle

fathers, but we know them. These fathers are not perfect, but they are good, honest, caring men, who live to provide for their families.

They are men who work long hours at jobs they may or may not like. They are the kind of men who drive straight from work in order to attend their kid's games, recitals, practices, and family dinners. They were not grumpy when they arrived. Tired, sure. Stressed, you bet. But glad to be there. Smiling. Laughing. These are solid men who are living in ways that show sacrificial love. They are our church members. They are men that provide for their family, and love their neighbors. At first glance this sounds pretty Jesus-y.

And yet, we could see that for these men, church was optional. Absolutely, they thought it was a good thing. But maybe a good thing interchangeable with going out on the boat, or a lazy Sunday morning in pajamas. These men would participate at our church's special events, but not routine events. These were great guys, models of fatherhood, professing to be followers of Christ… but, not fully engaged in the church. Dallas Willard observes,

> When our presentation of the gospel fails to do justice to this basic truth about the nature of human personality, Christianity inevitably becomes alienated from our actual daily existence. All that remains for it are a few "special" acts to be engaged in on rare occasions.[8]

Willard notes that the Christian life is usually separated from our normal, daily existence. He concludes that the Christian is incomplete because they are lacking behaviors, which he calls disciplines of the faith.[9] The inadequate commitment in the church, he observes, is not because someone is not conservative or liberal enough, or Protestant or Catholic enough; it is from a common weakness of not physically practicing the faith.

As men raised in the church why didn't these fathers consider church an essential part of providing for their children's future?

These men wanted their children to have a secure and stable future. They were professing Christians, and yet, they considered church an optional add-on.

---

[8] Willard 2004, p. 31 of 277, Kindle
[9] Ibid. p. 31 of 277, Kindle

We saw this reality in the life of our church. The Christian life was reserved for the "BIG" stuff, when medicine runs out, when society collapses, when people die; the "NOSTALGIA" stuff, after all "Christmas just doesn't feel like Christmas without the candlelight service;" or the "SPIRITUAL" stuff, alongside yoga and therapy, church offers options for the soul. For many, the Christian life was not a daily, lived experience.

How is it that well-meaning, faithful Christians fall into these traps? And how is it that someone can attend church their whole life, and still fall victim to these shallow versions of the gospel?

As Willard points out, the problem was not beliefs. It was not an issue of having the right thoughts. The issue was that, as a church, we were not providing a place for folks to physically practice the faith.

A New Idea - OptIN

One Friday night, we were eating dinner at a local restaurant. As married co-pastors, we don't do a very good job of leaving work at work. Which is why we were trying to figure out how to better equip our people to follow Jesus Christ. We were trying to figure out what we could do for the faithful church members that wanted more, or for the hesitant fathers needing more. Maybe new or 'better' ideas *about* God was not the solution for the frustrated faithful or the sporadic faithful.

We realized that the normal activities of church were meeting some needs, but they were falling short. We had holes, leaks, in our faith experience as a church and it was seen in the suffering of the faithful and in the lack of urgency in families that identified themselves as part of our church. What we were seeing is not unusual. It's a common struggle in most churches. What changed for us was that our personal connection to the church led us to take it personally as pastors. It is easier to blame the church than it is to wonder what we might do differently as leaders. It's easier, until you're too invested in the peopl to be ok blaming them.

Micaiah's father was a missionary and denominational director for decades in our denomination. He observed, when working with church revitalization, that churches in decline often were suffering from a leadership problem. The pastor and church board (elders) needed to improve with respect to their skills. The pastor needed to do a better job preaching, relating to people, managing their time. The elders needed to learn how to lead Bible studies, pray, relate to people, be kind and friendly.

He observed that the church was in decline because it was lacking people with skills. Often, once an assessment was made and the church's leadership informed as to what needed change, most refused to make any changes. They agreed others needed to change, but it never became personal. They were unwilling to learn or improve skills. In his experience, pastors were the least likely to consider improving their skills. They were glad to file the report and send the consultant on their merry way. Church revitalization requires that leaders learn new skills and effectively practice them. Church revitalization is humbling because people must change; they need to learn how to do things better.

People we loved were not thriving because of our shortcomings. It was literally our job to lead our church in their spiritual journey. If they were not on the right path, it was because we had not led them onto the right path. Because these were our people and we genuinely cared about them, we wanted them to experience more.

So, we grabbed a pen and paper napkin, and got to work. It was there that the initial concept of OptIN was drafted. We envisioned a 10-month program that led a small group through different practices of the faith: storytelling, prayer, worship, Sabbath, etc. We even populated a list of potential participants on that paper napkin.

It wasn't long after our paper-napkin vision that we heard about a grant opportunity that could help us fund different aspects of our project, namely, working with consultants. It was a small grant of $3,000. We were confident we would receive this funding, but our application was rejected. Needless to say, we were off to a slow start.

Micaiah, upon being rejected, decided that she simply wouldn't take "no" for an answer. We went to Princeton Seminary, after all, and surely we had connections to people who could help us. After a few phone calls, and some sound advice, we decided to proceed with our idea. We'd start a group in our church as a test to see what worked and what didn't.

We invited a pilot group of people from our church, and pitched OptIN to them. A half-dozen families came to our initial explanatory meeting. We had a group of all ages: 14 to 84, and everything in between. We pitched OptIN as a skills-based Christian formation class. We asked this group to commit to meeting every week for 10 months, with make-up classes in the event someone couldn't be there. Every class included homework, and vulnerability would be required. We were swinging for the fences with our first group.

For most of our pitch, we got blank stares and silence. Pushing through, we put most of the social capital we had amassed as their pastors on the line. They probably would have said no, except for one of those tough country women who are the pillars of so many communities. Martha, all of 4 foot 11 and 84 years old, said to the group, "I've spent a lot of time in my life on myself, investing in my family, taking care of everything else. I can afford to spend 10 months on God. I think we need to." She was the first to OptIN.

Martha's commitment meant that the rest of the group followed suit. In a profoundly humbling moment, our guinea pig group said yes.

(It should be noted – OptIN has come a long way since this first meeting. We no longer ask people for a 10-month commitment. We suggest they try one unit of OptIN, which is about six to eight sessions.)

Our paper-napkin vision for OptIN was a Christian formation program, designed from the start to practice, not teach, Christian skills. We suspected that better preaching and teaching would not form better Christians. Simply because there is a limit to inspiration. We suspected that simply changing the materials we were using in Sunday school, would again, not form better Christians. Simply because the Christian life is more than a right set of beliefs.

Our first guinea pig OptIN group was a failure in many ways. Ten months was too long of a time commitment. We spent too much of the class teaching, instead of practicing skills. We tried to cover every aspect of the Christian life, which was a bit like drinking from a fire hose. While it failed in these ways, it also changed the lives of our participants. We had life-long Christians break down in tears because they had never experienced Christian practices in this way. Some of our participants felt a true sense of belonging to the church as a byproduct of the communal nature of the group. Two young women realized their gifting for church-work, and began entertaining calls to ministry. One participant said, "I have been a Christian for a long time, but I didn't realize how much I had failed to include God in my daily way of life."

For the church system, OptIN produced leaders that we have since leaned on through different seasons of the church. It led to increased church involvement and a larger pool of volunteers. All of a sudden, people felt equipped to lead, to pray, to tell a testimony. The only reason they felt equipped was because we practiced those skills.

The name OptIN is based on the idea that to go deeper in faith we have to make a decision to opt-in to a set of practices that form the Christian life. OptIN is not a challenge for a greater commitment to faith; it is a methodology. It is not so much about opting-in to a new program, but instead, is about a *way of learning* that is not lecture or classroom based. The innovation of OptIN is not just finding the time to join a new church group, but is connecting people to a skills-based method of Christian formation. OptIN was designed to help people develop fundamental skills that unlock Christian flourishing.

We realize that for the faithful and for those struggling to be faithful, there is a disconnect in how they live a Christian life. For a meaningful Christian life, we need to *do* meaningful things, not just show up to be taught. We need to *do* God things, and not just know God things. This emphasis on *doing* highlights the need for action and experimentation. All Christians have the need for a skeletal framework of skills, habits, routines, and practices upon which a Christian can begin to move and live more naturally in the world. Christians need a discipleship program which involves practices that lead to Christian formation. The OptIN approach involves practicing new skills, going from simple to more complex. As the OptIN group practices together they talk about their experience. OptIN guides practice, instead of teaching content. Theology is only a consequence of the group interacting in their theological context.

No dancer learns to dance by reading a book. When Micaiah trained in ballet, they would spend hours doing work at the barre (handrail). After weeks, and months of skill development and practice, there would finally be a show. But first, they would plié and stretch and pirouette.

In church, people want to 'dance.' But no one teaches you how. You learn the value of 'dancing,' but you don't learn the skills needed to actually 'dance.' OptIN seeks to be a resource in this lane of skill development, so that individuals and churches can dance.

Over the years, we have launched new OptIN groups in our church. Eventually, we took our new methodology to the Lilly Foundation and were blessed to receive two grants to help us develop this idea. Lilly saw OptIN as a way to help churches and Christian families thrive. These funds have allowed us to expand into various churches to form OptIN groups. It has also allowed us to develop a family version of OptIN. At all stages of OptIN development, we see it as a research project. We develop units and ideas around the OptIN method, then we test it, refine it, and test it again. Try something. Fail. And then, try again.

Chapter 3 – The Core Units

We confidently promote OptIN methods to all Christians. We know that all Christian traditions, Protestant, Catholic, Orthodox, reformed, fundamentalist, progressive, conservative, and Pentecostals, etc. believe in the importance of Christian practices. In fact, spiritual disciplines are not unique to Christians. It is not enough to merely invite Christians to engage in Christian practices. This is not to discredit the good intentions or earnest desires of any individual Christian. It is a recognition that the practices that make up our faith are not necessarily Christian in their performance. The practice alone is not what makes us Christian. This is superficially obvious in that every world religion has some form of prayer and meditation, of gathering, and of worship. If the church were agnostic about the character of God, then the church would also be agnostic about our form of prayer. Christians profess particular beliefs, and Christian practices should be manifestations of those beliefs.

Diverse Christian Practices

The church is not agnostic about the character of God. Instead, the church is rooted in the particular action and revelation of Jesus. No Jesus, no church. No Holy Spirit, no church. Because the church has particular convictions about the character and action of God, the church cannot be agnostic about how the faith is practiced. For all practices, the church must shape and instruct engagement in various practices so that they are Christian practices. I would argue that the neglect of hands-on teaching of practices has led people who attend our churches to seek out other forms of spirituality, even non-Christian, to fill the void. So how do we distinguish Christian practices from non-Christian practices? What is the difference between a Hindu, Buddhist or Christian prayer?

This doesn't mean all practices must be identical. A framework for evaluating Christian practices already exists for the church. Quite early on, scripture is referred to as canon, from the Greek word *kanon* meaning 'rule' or 'measure.' It is not assumed that these texts are the only revelation from God. Scripture itself assumes the opposite, expecting the faithful to prophecy, to hear the Spirit, to be given words and wisdom and guidance. God's revelation is perfect, but our access and comprehension of this revelation is never perfect. Scripture, then, is not put forward as an exclusive act of revelation. It is a 'rule' or 'measure' for all subsequent revelation. God will continue speaking to God's church.

The church is to judge and understand this speech by the 'rule' given to us. As we realized early on when exploring how to revitalize our church through practices of the Faith, the study and teaching of the Bible and the Kingdom it presents is something the Church loves to do. In the case of setting boundaries for Christian practices, The Bible is the infallible rule for both faith and practice.

NT Wright and Michael Bird summarize this dynamic: "The early church had more than two categories of writings. It was never a matter of seeing everything as *either* 'inspired' *or* 'heretical'. Christian teachers recognized that there was a larger body of works that were, at least, para-canonical, useful to be read alongside the authorized body of normative Christian texts."[10] Such an approach to scripture is behind this advice from Augustine:

> The most skillful interpreter of the sacred writings, then, will be he who in the first place has read them all and retained them in his knowledge, if not yet with full understanding, still with such knowledge as reading gives,—those of them, at least, that are called *canonical*. For he will read the others with greater safety when built up in the belief of the truth, so that they will not take first possession of a weak mind, nor, cheating it with dangerous falsehoods and delusions, fill it with prejudices averse to a sound understanding.[11]

Because Christians locate truth in God, not in ourselves or our traditions or our hearts, the canonical writings of scripture set a foundation for understanding that enables proper perception and judgment of everything else, including ourselves, our beliefs and our practices. The truth of the canon allows us to recognize "dangerous falsehoods and delusions," that might otherwise creep in and deceive us. Just as beliefs can be heretical, practices can as well. OptIN is not about promoting practices for the sake of doing activities that makes us feel better. There are many self-help books that promote activities of mindfulness, finding oneself, or lowering anxiety. Our focus is imitating Christ and promoting practices based on beliefs about Jesus Christ that draw one to Christ.

Each OptIN unit provides a structure within which to practice these skills, and experiment within the supportive context of the group. We are all guided by the exemplar life of Christ and the Scriptures inspired by

---

[10] Wright, Bird 2019, p. 873

[11] Augustine, Bk 2. Chapter 8.12

God. On the other hand, OptIN is done within the context of a Christian church. Practices are done in the context of a culture, language and liturgical tradition. We emphasize to those who use OptIN that we are not promoting a particular Christian style or tradition. Christian practices are needed within all Christian styles and traditions.

Starting With the Basics

OptIN focuses on three core units: Story, Prayer, and Worship. Without practice in these three areas, an individual is limited in their ability to fully participate in the life of the church. When these are treated as simple skills—either in the sense that they are simple and easy to do, or in the sense that they are basic and cannot be subdivided—only those who are naturally disposed or gifted will be able to enter into them. They are not simple in either sense.

First, story, prayer, and worship are all complex and difficult to do well. This does not mean that an imperfect performance is somehow unfaithful. It does mean that Christians can and should continue to grow in these complex tasks for their whole lives. Which is why it's good news that they aren't simple in the second sense.

Story, prayer, and worship can all be divided into component parts. Let me remind you that Daniel Coyle's book on learning he explains, "Every skill is built out of smaller pieces—what scientists call chunks. Chunks are to skills what letters of the alphabet are to language. Alone, each is nearly useless, but when combined into bigger chunks… they can build something complex and beautiful."[12]

Story, prayer, and worship are each complex activities made up of a constellation of smaller skills. For example, telling stories of God's activity in our lives requires numerous sub-skills; an individual must internalize true stories of God from tradition and scripture; learn to recognize God's presence; know their personal history; have the humility to submit their history to God's story; apply stories of scripture and and tradition to recognize God's presence in their history; and the ability to write their history with God's presence correctly identified into a coherent story. Telling a story of God's activity can be done with a deficiency in any of these components, but that telling of a story is more susceptible to "dangerous falsehoods and delusions."

---

[12] Coyle 2012, p. 45

In explaining how these fundamentals are treated in hotbeds of learning, Coyle describes, "Each fundamental, no matter how humble-seeming, is introduced as a precise skill of huge importance, taught via a series of vivid images, and worked on over and over until it is mastered. The vital pieces are built, rep by careful rep."[13]

OptIN units provide a map for practicing these different activities, developing fundamental capacities that enable deeper and more complex engagements. In addition to practicing the basics, the core units introduce the OptIN trade school method of Christian formation. We have stated that our recourses present and model a method of Christian formation that we hope will inform church leaders to do their own versions and variations of hands-on skill development. OptIN resources that we developed are a means to an end. The end goal is that churches intentionally find ways to teach Christian disciplines by hands-on practice. Our resources illustrate what we are talking about. We believe practice and skill development can revitalize the Church.

Building Faithful Stories

In his book *Moral, Believing, Animals*, Christian Smith argues that human beings are inescapably and foundationally narrative creatures. Stories are not just an artistic way of arranging the facts of our lives. "In a narrative world not all 'facts' matter. What matters is the more significant story running through, over, and under 'the facts,' the story that itself constitutes what is a fact, what it is that matters."[14] Whether George Washington is a hero or a rebellious insurrectionist is not just a matter of emphasis or preference. It is a not a "fact" we can discover by reading the history books. Both of these are true, depending on the story they are embedded in. The story shapes and determines the meaning and value of different facts.

> "The stories we tell are not mere entertainment. Nor do they simply suggest for us some general sense of our heritage. Our stories fully encompass and define our lives. They situate us in reality itself, by elaborating the contours of fundamental moral order, comprising sacred and profane, in narrative form, and placing us too as actors within the larger drama. Our individual and collective lives come to

---

[13] Ibid., p. 22
[14] Smith 2021, p. 66

have meaning and purpose insofar as they join the larger cast of characters enacting, reenacting, and perpetuating the larger narrative. It is by finding ourselves placed within a particular drama that we come to know our role, our part, our lines in life—how we are to act, why, and what meaning that has in a larger scheme of reality."[15]

Stories don't just respond to our experience of the world. They also shape our experience of the world. Is a dog a potentially dangerous animal that should be avoided, or a working animal bred for a specific purpose, or a member of the family, or like chicken and cows is it good for eating? These aren't scientific questions. They are narrative questions.

> *One participant couldn't name where God was active in her life. When she told the group that, they stepped in with God-sighting after God-sighting. They helped her see.*
> **Pastor in Alabama**

Recognizing that stories shape our experience of the world does not mean facts don't matter. There are a variety of stories that can fit people's experiences of dogs, but when people try to tell a story about bears or chimpanzees being good pets, those stories end differently. Reality pushes back.

As the church, we are telling a story that God is living and active in the world. We tell a story that the Holy Spirit is shaping us into the people of God. We tell stories about individuals that they are made in the image of God, that they are gifted for the work of the world, that creation is good and beautiful. We tell these stories, recognizing that they are in competition with other stories that are seeking to define people's realities differently.

When the church fails to take seriously that our perception of reality is shaped by our stories, we fail to realize how the stories we are raised in shape our perception of the faith. In an individualist and consumerist culture, the faith is easily reduced to a personal pursuit (me and Jesus) or a service provided (God just wants me to be happy, so church is about making my life easier).

Tim Suttle explains, "Stories make mental maps for us, maps of our own lives. They tell us who we are and help us make sense of the world

---

[15] Ibid., p. 78

around us."¹⁶ The "map" image is instructive. Stories aren't something artificial layered onto something real. A good map helps a user navigate and understand reality. A map of London helps you know what's in London, helps you navigate from place to place, and gives you a better sense of the city as a whole. It is a different experience than walking the city. But a good map helps you understand the city as you walk it. A good story helps us know each other and ourselves.

Like a good map, a good story helps us find ourselves. A faithful Christian story helps us find ourselves, not just in the world, but in God's world. Because stories have that kind of power, good stories can give our lives meaning and purpose. Beautiful stories lead people to make incredible sacrifices. Bad stories can confuse us or obscure our sense of truth, of God's presence, of what is good and beautiful and worthwhile. Storytelling is an important aspect of the Christian life because stories are how we see and interpret our world.

> *Our first-generation Japanese Christians shared about the cost of following Jesus. Many were kicked out of their homes and lost their families. It's vital for our community to hear and honor these stories. Having their stories heard was important for them being seen and known in our congregation.*
>
> **Pastor in Kentucky**

As God's people are sitting in camp after walking out of slavery in Egypt, Moses tells them to commemorate that day every year by cleaning out all yeast and eating unleavened bread. Then, "On that day tell your son, 'I do this because of what the Lord did for me when I came out of Egypt.' This observance will be for you like a sign on your hand and a reminder on your forehead that this law of the Lord is to be on your lips."

Telling the story, year after year, is a way of reminding all of God's people that we serve a God who is living and active, who saved our ancestors and still saves today. Without telling out stories, we join the wrong part of the story: "They believed his words, they sang his praise. But they soon forgot his works; they did not wait for his counsel."¹⁷

---

¹⁶ Suttle 2014, p. 100

¹⁷ Psalm 105:12-13

Goal of OptIN Story Unit:

> "As a society, we've lost the ability to tell stories. People were grateful for the chance to practice this skill again."
> **Pastor in Georgia**

The OptIN story unit helps participants "build" faithful stories. Stories are most commonly, "told," and the Building Stories unit does help participants tell stories. But telling a story is not the first step. Our stories don't form themselves as we go through life.

Instead, we teach participants to think of stories like building a house. The verb helps participants understand the sort of work we are about to do. Below are some of the implications we are drawing on when we "build" stories, instead of merely telling them.

1. **Building depends on a foundation:** Jesus tells us that those who build a house on his teachings and his commands are like a house on a firm foundation (Mt. 7). In Luke's version, it's a man who digs, and digs deeply to lay a foundation. This foundation isn't found inside an individual's heart. It isn't a personal foundation. The foundation is Jesus. Because our stories shape how we perceive ourselves and our reality, an individual cannot tell themselves into this story. We have to be told into it. Above all, this is done by God's word in scripture. But scripture is God's gift to the church, and it is the church that tells people a new story and gives them a new foundation. So Paul can say, "You are God's building. Because of God's grace to me, I have laid the foundation like an expert builder. Now others are building on it. But whoever is building on this foundation must be very careful. For no one can lay any foundation other than the one we already have —Jesus Christ."[18]

> "So many times I hear, 'I've gone to church with you for 20 years and never knew THAT.'"
> **Pastor in Kentucky**

2. **Building requires supplies:** A building cannot be built from ideas. It requires whatever materials will be used for the foundation, structure, walls, the roof, and windows. It might need concrete, rebar, lumber, siding, bricks, and shingles. When it comes to telling our own stories, the facts of our history and context are the supplies we have. Lots of energy can go to wishing for different materials—a different history, a different context—but this isn't how God tends to work. God

---

[18] 1 Corinthians 3:10-11 (NLT).

> *The Stories Unit created space for a man from Trinidad, as well as a Black man and several white men from [the US] to hear each other's stories and admit, "I was raised to think this way about you, and I need to acknowledge I wasn't raised right."*
>
> **Pastor in Alabama**

grows new plants from stumps, and stirs up old bones. This is new life, and new stories, from less-than-ideal supplies.

3. **Building doesn't happen by magic:** there is only one way that a pile of lumber becomes the framed-in walls of a house. People take hammers and nails and do the work. Stories are the same. We don't just find good stories sitting around. Facts don't magically become stories. Our past doesn't magically receive a shape, much less a Christian shape. We don't automatically get to know each other by sitting near each other on Sunday mornings. It takes time and attention, telling and retelling stories, to give them a shape. To know ourselves and each other as God does takes work.

4. **Building is personal:** there is a reason your house or apartment or room feels like home to you. It is yours. It has your mark on it. The world of the church is full of beautiful, compelling, and emotional stories. They are everywhere. But they are told by brilliant, world-class communicators (usually preachers or theologians). Other people can visit these stories. But they won't be, "my story." Hearing stories is important and formational work. Something different happens when we tell stories, and when other people hear our stories. This act of building a story, then telling a story, and having the church validate your story, is like claiming a room in the household of God.

5. **Building poorly has consequences:** the world is full of poorly designed houses, and poorly designed houses have consequences. This helps us recognize the consequences of living with poorly built stories. A poorly arranged house could be uncomfortable, might not have spaces for people to gather, or might have terrible light. All of these make that house feel less "at home," less comfortable. A poorly arranged story can do the same thing, constricting facts or distorting realities in uncomfortable ways. A poorly built house can be dangerous. A poorly built story can be as well, pushing people into self-perceptions or activities that are destructive to themselves or others. It is a story that leads one nation or people-group to describe

other human beings as being less-worthwhile, and it is a better story that is necessary to reject this sort of claim.

The OptIN Story unit is aimed at two concrete goals: 1) Telling a story of God's activity in your life and 2) Listening to others tell stories about God's activity in their lives. The story of scripture is true whether or not we realize it. In learning to tell our stories through scripture, we come to see its truth, not just as a theoretical rule book, but as a living and active gift from God to the church. Likewise, our new identities in Christ are true whether or not we experience them as true. But in narrating our new identities to a community, and in having them hear and affirm our stories, the stories come to shape how we see ourselves and our world. Without this personal act of narration, the stories easily remain outside of us. They float like ideas, instead of seeds that can put down roots and grow fruit.

The Christian anthropologist Paul Hiebert[19] explains that humans find meaning from three areas of narratives: First, "my story" (biography); second, "group stories"; and third, "the cosmic story." We see all of these narratives modeled in Scripture, and we all have these stories inside of us, whether or not we realize it.

While we have primarily emphasized building stories, it matters profoundly that our stories are heard and received. In this age of distraction, helping congregants attend well is an area of growing focus for us. As a Pastor in Georgia noted, "We could strengthen the program with a session on how to listen well and ask thoughtful questions. Many participants struggled with that."

If a participant tells a story and no one bothers to listen, that indifference also tells a story. "We're not interested." Or, "That story isn't valuable." By making space for people's stories, and by listening to them attentively, and maybe even by preserving parts of the story to share in the future, the church is telling a different story. "You are part of our family, and we see God living and active in you.'

> I had a visitor to our church join my story unit, and I was worried about him fitting in. The sharing and receiving of stories helpd integrate him into the congregation so well. He knows he belongs.
> **Pastor in Mississippi**

---

[19] Hiebert 2000, loc. 1,959-2,007 of 8,124, Kindle

One pastor shared with us, "I have a group of older guys doing OptIN with me. They aren't all members of my church, but they are all part of a breakfast group that meets at Hardees on Mondays, Wednesday, and Friday. OptIN is connecting enough with their lives that they are getting into the material at Hardees and discussing it with their friends before they even show up for our meeting together. From me struggling to get investment in Christian Ed. to this has been... an adjustment."

Practicing Prayer

Obviously, prayer is a central theme of Christian formation. And there are tons of existing resources on paryer. Jesus taught his disciples to pray. He and his disciples participated in the daily rhythms of morning and evening prayer that shaped—and still shape—Jewish life. He prayed the Psalms and Deuteronomy 6. But he also built something new on this foundation. He taught them to pray the words, "Our Father in heaven, holy is your name..." In this prayer, he invited them to be with God in a new reality that he was inviting them into. We know he modeled solitude, silence, and fasting, praying with the community, praying with persistence. We know he modeled prayer that isn't answered in the garden of Gethsemane.

> *Prayer, although it might seem intuitive, has been a challenging practice for me... Teaching and practicing prayer have become increasingly vital as I deepen my faith.*
> **Pastor in Kentucky**

In all this, we see that Jesus never assumed his disciples should intuitively know how to pray. In fact, he explicitly assumed the opposite. He warned them about dysfunctional modes of prayer that aren't truthful to who God is in Matthew 6, and about inconstant prayer in Luke 18. If we are called to model our lives around the life of Christ, this doesn't just mean praying. It means learning to pray from Jesus.

Will Willimon and Stanley Hauerwas explore the importance of this learning posture in their book, Lord, Teach Us: The Lord's Prayer & the Christian Life. They acknowledge that, "The notion of the necessity of being taught to pray may sound odd. It is supposed to sound odd in a society that worships individual autonomy, freedom, and detachment, a culture that has taught us to live so that we are determined by no tradition, that we are accountable to nothing outside the self... turning our lives into a mere matter of consumer preference."[20] Our world teaches us that the truth and value for any practice is our personal preference. This consumer mentality assumes we should pray in whatever way feels right, whatever way we like.

Committing to follow Jesus is an act of defiance against this deficient worldview. To follow Jesus is to decide that Jesus is, "the way, the truth, and the life." This requires letting go of my way, my truth, and my life.

Following Jesus means letting go of our way of praying because Jesus has a more truthful way to pray. Returning to Willimon and Hauerwas, "There are all kinds of prayer, but prayer as Jesus taught is a peculiar kind of activity based upon the life, death, and resurrection of Jesus. We don't decide to become Christians and then find that the Lord's Prayer is a helpful means of expressing our faith. We don't choose this prayer; it chooses us. It reaches out to us, forms us, invites us into the adventure called discipleship."[21]

To begin praying without this formation and model wouldn't mean God can't hear us. It would mean that our conversation with God—our speaking and our silence—are defined by our understanding of reality, our understanding of God, our understanding of what is important and urgent and worth saying and worth asking for. Submitting to Jesus as a teacher in prayer means that God can be healing our hearts and imaginations from these deformed desires.

We don't decide to be Christian and automatically begin praying as Christians. We have to be taught to pray. Prayer is bending our lives toward God, so we practice over and over again bringing ourselves into God's presence, speaking and listening.

When the disciples asked Jesus about prayer, he did not tell them to go off and sit quietly until something spiritual came to their minds. He did not ask them, "Well, how do you feel about God?" He said, "Pray like this. 'Our Father…..'"

We, who are accustomed to thinking of prayer as a good strategy for getting what we want ("The family who prays together stays together") and an appropriate opening for football games and important civic meetings, may be surprised that we must be taught to pray. This prayer is

---

[20] Willimon, Hauerwas, 1996, p. 6

[21] Ibid., p. 6

not for getting what we want but rather for bending our wants toward what God wants. In praying this prayer we become the people God has called us to be in Jesus.

Augustine explains, in reference to the Lord's Prayer, that when we say, "Hallowed be Thy name" we are challenging ourselves to esteem God. When we say "Thy kingdom come" we are not forcing God to send it. We are trying to open our lives and our hearts to God's kingdom. And when we pray, "Thy will be done" we are praying for God's help that our imperfect hearts and wills might obey God, even as the angels in heaven obey God.[22] The Lord's Prayer gives us direction; it is the bending of our wants toward those of God.

Goal of OptIN Prayer Unit:

> One parent told me, 'We never prayed together before this. Now our kids remind us at dinner.' That's a beautiful kind of reversal.
> **Pastor in Alabama**

One reflection we've heard from OptIN participants is that the prayer unit is less immediately impactful than the story unit. Telling stories can immediately connect us to others in an emotionally powerful way. You build a story and, voila! You can see it. Prayer, we realized as we practiced, is work!

This unit is not called, "Building Prayers," because that isn't how prayer works. Prayer cannot force God's presence. That would be magic. We also chose not to use the metaphor of a conversation for prayer. This image is most people's operative understanding of prayer, and with good reason. There is helpful explanatory power in calling prayer a conversation. But relying so heavily on this model also conceals ways prayer is not like other sorts of conversations.

1. **Prayer is like a conversation:** Prayer is talking to God and listening to God, individually and in communities. Like conversation, inattention makes prayer shallow and ineffective. Like a conversation, honest speech in prayer depends on honest self-knowledge. Like a conversation, an intimate connection with God will depend on a truthful understanding of God and God's character. Maybe someone you knew when you were young still insists on engaging you like you were that you age. It makes you want to say, "That's not who I am!"

---

[22] Augustine, Book XCCC, Sec. 21

That feelings is how God feels when we insist on treating God *how we imagine God should be* instead of how God really is.

2. **Prayer is like joining an *ongoing* and *communal* conversation:** When we pray, we are joining God's conversation with God's people. It is always joining an in-progress conversation. Some of this conversation is recorded in scripture. Some of it is taking place right now, as the body of Christ around the world calls out to God, listens to God, prays for us and pleads for our prayers. Prayer is never just us and the Father. We know this because our prayers are lifted up to God by the Holy Spirit, which intercedes on our behalf.[23] This same Spirit is lifting the prayers of believers around the world and throughout time. If that isn't enough, we know the communal nature of prayer mattered to Jesus. He gave us the "our Father," not the, "my Father." We can only pray the "our Father," because Jesus has invited us to join his church.

> *People were afraid to pray out loud… but by the end [of the unit], they were just doing it. It created a safe and invitational space to take that risk—and to discover prayer as something that can be simple and real.*
>
> **Pastor in Alabama**

3. **We can't see God:** our world is undergoing a fundamental transformation in communication. For nearly all of human history, we primarily communicated face to face. We are wired to communicate face to face. Increasingly, our connection and communication is happening online. Communicating in this way, it's easier to ignore someone's feelings, their context, their reaction to whatever we might like to say. It's harder to maintain focus on the conversation. It's harder to understand what exactly they meant without tone and bodily expressions. It's harder to feel grounded in our connection with them and easier to drift off into insecurity when we aren't physically together. Prayer can struggle from all these same ambiguities and challenges. It is easy to treat God

> *We used the OptIN prayer cards during worship, and it gave even our more hesitant members a place to begin. We realized: sometimes people just need the words handed to them first.*
>
> **Pastor in Alabama**

---

[23] Romans 8:26

like a distant and de-personified recipient of our "prayer" instead of a living and active conversation partner. It is easy to miss how God feels, God's context, God's reaction. It is easy to pray without feeling grounded in our connection with God.

4. **God is not a normal conversation partner:** there are no other people we've met who came with the warning, "Listen, you can't look on my face or you'll die." God is perfect. This is perfect in holiness, in goodness, in truth. Which means, entering more deeply into God's presence in prayer also means entering more deeply into holiness, goodness, and truth. Conversations are immediate, and we don't think of them as limited in this way. But perhaps like a child listening to an adult conversation, our ability to engage God in prayer is limited by our maturity in the faith.

5. **Prayer is also like a journey:** Like a journey, it is possible to get lost in prayer. We can get lost in our concerns or sins or confusion. It's easier to take a journey when we have a map, so getting familiar with maps like the Lord's Prayer and the prayers of the saints can help us find routes deeper into God's presence, or routes from unfamiliar or challenging life circumstances. Like a journey, there are obstacles in prayer. Like a journey, sometimes prayer is about carrying someone or something with us. There are ways we can better and more faithfully carry a person or situation into God's presence, including ways that let God change us and send us back as a gift to the person in need. Like a journey, prayer takes time. A lifetime of prayer should move our hearts closer to God. We should pray regularly, when nothing is wrong, so the route into God's presence is familiar.

> I used to think repetition might bore people—but it actually helped build trust. Prayer became a rhythm instead of a performance.
> **Pastor in Alabama**

6. **Prayer is also like a garden:** Like a garden, prayer suffers when our hearts and lives are full of weeds. Confessing and uprooting sins from our life makes room for God's word to grow in us. This sort of spirituality is especially prevalent in John's gospel and letters. Like a garden, prayer benefits from a routine that makes sure important practices happen regularly. Watering a garden when it feels right might work, if the climate is friendly and it's raining regularly. But when the sun gets hot, which is precisely the image Jesus gives us for shallow rooted plants in Matthew 13, if we aren't watering regularly, our prayer lives dry up. Finally, like a garden, prayer produces fruit

and beauty. We can and should expect our prayer lives to bear fruit. God's presence is awe inspiring. God is beautiful. God is true. This isn't just about communication. As we spend more time resting in the reality of God's presence, we are changed.

> *[After praying the Lord's Prayer line by line with silence in between] I prayed that pray my whole life but didn't know it could do that. I swore I couldn't sit and pray for 5 minutes, but when you called time I thought, "No! Not yet!"*
> **Participant in Alabama**

We've called this unit "Practicing Prayer" because learning to pray more deeply is a bit like starting to exercise. From one day to the next, things look more or less the same. There is not the same immediate payoff. If prayer is understood as a mere matter of desire or will, then practice is not necessary. But praying doesn't mean we suddenly become disembodied creatures. Our prayer lives are affected by our attention. If we lose the muscle to sit in attentive silence, how can we hear God's voice? If we are distracted in prayer, we don't magically attend to God's presence. Our minds lead us elsewhere. Training and preparing our hearts and minds doesn't earn us access to God's presence. But this training does allow us to more deeply attend to the free gift of God's presence we've been given in Jesus.

> *[On praying the Lord's Prayer with pauses] They loved it. They were so jazzed about preparing to pray in that way... it slows the mind down and opens the heart."*
> **Pastor in Alabama**

This sort of training is not always exciting. Returning again and again to God's presence, following the well-worn paths of prayer, can be routine. A routine prayer life can be a danger. It can mean we are going through the motions without actually bringing ourselves into God's presence. But without routine, our prayer lives will be stuck in the shallows.

Hauerwas and Willimon help explain this counterintuitive dynamic. "Most of the really important things we do in life, we do out of habit. We eat, sleep, make love, shake hands, hug our children out of habit. Some things in life are too important to be left up to chance. Some things in life are too difficult to be left up to spontaneous desire—things like telling people that we love them or praying to God. So we do them out of habit."[24]

The OptIN prayer unit tackles those difficult but crucial tasks of practicing prayer—building skills and stretching abilities—when the group is gathered together. The time to stretch our comfort with silence, or get familiar with a new prayer tool, or explore confession, is not by yourself on a busy Tuesday morning or when you know that dinner is almost ready and you're worried about it burning. Those are fine times to pray. Those are lousy times to experiment and stretch in prayer.

> One woman with neurodivergence told me after a guided silence, 'It was quieter in my brain.' That's huge.
> **Pastor in Alabama**

Just like any team, the time to push and stretch and experiment is when we're gathered together with the support of a leader and others who share our goal.

As a unit, the Practicing Prayer materials cannot give someone a prayer habit or routine. Supporting building routines is an area we are still experimenting in. But it does give people skills and tools that enable them to step more deeply into the life of prayer that Jesus invites the church into. OptIN's Practicing Prayer Unit introduces people to new and meaningful ways to pray.

Rehearsing Worship

There are many familiar critiques of worship in scripture. In Amos, God tells the people, "I hate, I despise your religious festivals; your assemblies are a stench to me. Even though you bring me burnt offerings and grain offerings, I will not accept them. Though you bring choice fellowship offerings, I will have no regard for them. Away with the noise of your songs! I will not listen to the music of your harps. But let justice roll on like a river, righteousness like a never-failing stream!"[25]

Critiques like this are often mobilized to suggest that the problem was inauthentic worship. As Jesus says, "Yet a time is coming and has now come when the true worshipers will worship the Father in the Spirit and

---

[24], Hauerwas, Willimon 1996, p. 7

[25] Amos 5:21-24

in truth, for they are the kind of worshipers the Father seeks. God is spirit, and his worshipers must worship in the Spirit and in truth."[26]

But, "Spirit and truth," is not the same as "authentic." More precisely, an urgent question confronting worship leaders and planners today is, "to what should worship be authentic?" To my personal desires and preferences? To contemporary styles and language? To traditional styles and language? Authentic to what?

The book of Hebrews helps us understand what Jesus meant by "Spirit and truth."

> "It was necessary, then, *for the copies of the heavenly things* to be purified with these sacrifices, but the heavenly things themselves with better sacrifices than these. For Christ did not enter a sanctuary made with human hands that was only *a copy of the true one*; he entered heaven itself, now to appear for us in God's presence."[27] [Italics added for emphasis.]

Jesus doesn't exceed the stale traditions of temple worship. Jesus fulfills the temple worship, which was a truthful copy of the heavenly reality. Faithful worship isn't about being authentic to what is in our hearts. It is about authentically participating in the true thing Jesus has accomplished:

> Therefore, brothers and sisters, since we have confidence to enter the Most Holy Place by the blood of Jesus, by a new and living way opened for us through the curtain, that is, his body, and since we have a great priest over the house of God, let us draw near to God with a sincere heart and with the full assurance that faith brings, having our hearts sprinkled to cleanse us from a guilty conscience and having our bodies washed with pure water. Let us hold unswervingly to the hope we profess, for he who promised is faithful.[28]

Worship must always be faithfully rooted in Jesus. It must conform to the image of Jesus. It must take place within the work of Jesus. Because the only way there is to enter the Most Holy Place is through Jesus. In this vein, the critique in Amos is not that God's people weren't participating

---

[26] John 4:23-24
[27] Hebrews 9:23-24
[28] Hebrews 10:19-23

in worship with their whole hearts. It's not that they weren't being faithful to the tradition, either. They were doing what God had told them to do in worship. They were engaging in the modes of worship God had commanded them to engage in. We have no reason to assume their hearts weren't fully in the worship they were offering. But their lives outside of worship contradicted the truth of God when they were gathered to worship.

Worship is not primarily self-expression. Worship is when the people of God come together as living sacrifices—offering our hearts and minds and lives to be conformed to the truth of who Jesus is and what he has done.[29] It does require earnestness and authenticity, as we offer ourselves completely to God. Understood in this way, worship is like a focused or condensed version of the Christian life. "Worship thus becomes a kind of performance before the performance, a preparation beforehand for whatever witness the church might be called upon to give. Being schooled in the basic rhythms and movements that constitute Christian faith means that the church's witness is more than something spoken, debated, written about, discussed; it is a faith that is enacted, performed, fleshed out. In order for such a witness to be faithful and true, in order for it to be convincing, the church must be attuned to the times."[30]

When we gather to worship, we gather to ascribe worth to the Triune God. We do things: bow, sing, kneel, speak, listen, pass peace, confess, forgive. All of things are according to the truth of who God is revealed to be. Doing these things, even and maybe especially when we would rather not, is ascribing worth to God.

Worship can, and often is, adjusted to match the abilities or understandings of participants. This sort of evangelistic impulse is common, but not without cost. "No matter how well meant the efforts are to turn worship into entertainment, the result is the sentimental perversion of worship that fails to provide any resistance to the ugliness of our surrounding culture—an ugliness, perhaps, nowhere more apparent than in the unbridled licentiousness of people unashamed of their greed."[31]

---

[29] Romans 12: 1-2
[30] Hauerwas 2004, p. 98
[31] Ibid., p. 161

The Rehearsing Worship unit attempts to stay agnostic on things like, "the worship wars." In doing so, we try to focus on what is necessary for intentional and attentive participation in worship. This means supporting and learning from both the ancient and modern wings of these conflicts. "When the liturgy becomes art understood in this modern sense, the church cannot help but be a museum of a beautiful but exotic past. That is why it is crucial, particularly in light of the challenges of modernity, that the beauty of the liturgy not be separated from the goodness of the One worshiped; nor can the goodness of lives of virtue be devoid of the beauty endowed by the Holy Spirit. The lives formed through the liturgy must at once be beautiful and good, reflecting the beauty and goodness of the One alone who is perfectly beautiful and good. The beauty and goodness of such lives have an end not as some further accomplishment but constitutive of lives well lived."[32]

Craig Dykstra invites his readers to, "Suppose that practices central to Christian life are conditions under which various kinds and forms of knowledge emerge - knowledge of God, of ourselves, and of the world; knowledge that is not only personal but also public… practices deserve a pivotal place in Christian formation, theological study, and theological education."[33]

More simply, there are things we can know only on the other side of having lived them. Worship opens us to such realities. We must engage in practices before we understand them, because the realities we encounter through these practices are the reason they are important. As we rehearse worship, we participate in doing things that reveal God. Worship is revelatory.

Dykstra goes on to note the importance of learning practices through mentors putting the practice in context.[34] This means we learn to worship by watching people worship. We learn how to worship through grief by attending funerals and seeing others worship through their grief. We learn to worship when we don't feel God by worshipping alongside others who don't feel God. Above all, we learn to worship by attending to the life, death, and resurrection of Jesus, and how that is being put into flesh in our midst.

---

[32] Hauerwas 2004, pp. 162-163
[33] Murphy, Et. al. 2003, p. 175
[34] Ibid., pp. 176–77

Our worship of God is best understood when we practice the elements of worship, together.

Goal of OptIN Worship Unit:

Worship marks the time of Christ that breaks into "our" time. We set aside worship as a time for God to interrupt and be present. As believers, we want to be ready when God arrives. Worship, then, is not just a way of filling up for the week, or being renewed so we can get back to life. Worship is the main event.

By calling this unit, "Rehearsing Worship," we are trying to recognize that these actions are not familiar. Singing a song as a gift to God is different than singing along to a song on the radio. Sitting in church is different than sitting in a concert. Forgiving someone can be something that takes some preparation. Hearing God speak through a sermon is different than picking out favorite lines from a TED talk. The activities of worship are strange. If we don't rehearse the motions, get familiar with the goals, anticipate what God might do, then our participation in worship can stumble.

Without intentionality, worship gets defined by these more familiar practices of being at a concert, or watching TV, or listening to an inspirational speech. But it isn't "not" these things. Here are some models we lean on for worship:

1. **Worship is like the temple (heaven on earth):** drawing from our exploration of Hebrews above, it's important to remember that when the church gathers to worship, we are gathering to embody a heavenly reality. The congregation is an embassy of heaven on earth. Like the temple, our worship service should represent divine realities in human form. Like the temple, worship should be built around the presence of God. This insight is especially grating in a consumer society that expects everything to be built around our personal preferences and desires. Like the temple, worship should be marked by offerings ascending toward God. One of these offerings

> *Incorporating stations in worship—candle lighting, intercessory prayer tables, Lectio Divina—has deepened relationships with God and created sacred moments.*
> **Pastor in Kentucky**

is gathering together. We gather with people we wouldn't have chosen, because God chose them. Finally, like the temple, worship should be distinct from the world around it while being built of local materials (sanctified for Godly purposes). This means worship should be of the people, and should include the people's gifts. But the gifts are sanctified by God's presence, not simply baptized without transformation.

> *Before, we had a handful of folks who participated in worship. After integrating OptIN resources, we saw wider engagement, especially during the storytelling moments.*
>
> **Pastor in Alabama**

2. **Worship is like a bootcamp**—drawn from Samuel Wells and Stanley Hauerwas' book on Christian ethics, this image emphasizes that worship is not just something we do. It is something we do that is supposed to change us.

> *I've been guiding a spiritual practice each week in worship, and I also put the practice in the bulletin. That way I'm equipping my congregants to take it with them into their week.*
>
> **Pastor in Kentucky**

A. Bootcamp assumes that individuals who cannot do certain tasks can be trained and exercised until they are able to do those tasks. Worship should comfort and reassure us. It can and should also be challenging, as it stretches us into the image of Jesus.

B. Bootcamp assumes a mission that participants want to fulfill more than they want to meet personal needs or momentary desires. Helping people internalize the mission of worship—glorification of God—enables them to recognize and set aside personal preferences or grievances for the sake of the larger mission.

C. Bootcamp recognizes the importance of community for motivation and behavior change. You travel to bootcamp because no one would put themselves through all of that. Because of human psychology, it's much easier to submit as someone else puts you through something like that for the sake of a worthwhile outcome.

D. Finally, bootcamp recognizes that virtues are habits of character, not a matter of willpower of desire. Character takes time to develop. No one is born with it. But worship gives us opportunities to do and say the right thing, even when we don't want to.

3. **Worship is like a rehearsal**—Our favorite image for worship, it gives us agency in preparing to encounter God. We believe God is faithful to arrive. We believe worship is God's family reunion. Rehearsal is how we get ready.

> One member told me that after rehearsing worship, 'It felt like we were worshiping as real people, not trying to put on a show.' That's a big win.
>
> **Pastor in Alabama**

   A. We cannot affect when God will "arrive", but we can be more or less prepared for the real thing when it occurs. Rehearsing different activities and moments of worship means we know where to be looking for God's presence, and alerts us to what distractions or mistakes we should be on-guard against.
   B. Rehearsal involves practicing particular skills and movements until they are second nature so that they can be performed without thought. "Without thought" does carry risk, as people can worship while writing their grocery list. "Without thought" also describes the dancer who is so familiar with the steps, that they can be fully present to their dance partner instead of trying to remember if they should move their left foot or their right. Practicing core movements of worship means that they feel natural and familiar when they are done "for real" in worship, allowing us to attend to God and one another.
   C. Importance doesn't come from novelty, it comes from the EVENT itself as a moment of significance. This image leans on the previous two, where the reason to fully participate in worship is not because I feel something. It's because God is present in the worship, and the worship itself is true. What we want to experience is the truth of God's presence with us, God's family. By participating in worship, by choosing to fully attend to it, we are participating in the truth.
   D. Private rehearsal imitates the event, but understands this is not a substitute for the event. Personal preparation is necessary to play "my role." If the individual is not prepared—or present—the group event suffers. Likewise, if the individual confuses personal preparation with the main event, they have missed the point.

Elements of worship can be rehearsed, and practiced. It doesn't mean that you can't just show up to a worship service and participate; you can.

It doesn't mean that God will or won't show up in a supernatural way in a particular service; that is something we cannot control. BUT, when we rehearse worship, our experience of worship is deeper, it's richer.

The goal of the OptIN Worship Unit is to help participants rehearse the different elements of worship, and to strengthen the bonds between people in the OptIN group as a way to strengthen the bonds of the worshipping community.

Chapter 4 – OptIN Methodology

In a typical OptIN class, a group (6-25 people) gathers for 6-8 weeks around one particular unit: Story, Prayer, or Worship. This class meets weekly to practice the sub-skills required by each unit, and all of the units culminate with an activity that puts all the sub-skills together. Story concludes by each participant sharing with the class one story of God's activity in his/her life. Prayer concludes with a guided prayer vigil. Worship concludes with participants bringing their gifts together in order to lead a Sunday morning worship service.

These groups are intergenerational, made up of confirmed members and up. Ideally, OptIN groups include whole family units whenever possible. After the 6(ish) week unit is over, the group can disband or keep going through a different skill. Because these are skills-based units, they can be repeated over time: after all, we all have more than one story to share.

These groups meet at a place and time that works for that group. Meaning, these groups could meet during an already existing Sunday School hour, or they can set up an evening weekly meeting. Meals can be included or not. An OptIN unit could take the place of an already existing Bible Study for a season. The units are all short enough that they can be included in the church calendar when it works best for that congregation.

While this is the ideal model for OptIN, OptIN as a methodology can be used in many different ways. We have had youth groups run OptIN units, we have had a small group of 4-5 people run OptIN units. We have adapted the OptIN Being Church unit for use in a conference setting (of 500 people). We have adapted the OptIN Practicing Prayer unit for use as a VBS curriculum, centered around teaching children how to pray.

> *I had people who had checked out of Sunday School, but I convinced them to try this. They began hesitantly but ended up sharing personal stories. The laughter was good. They crying was too. This unit made it possible.*
> **Pastor in Alabama**

We have hosted OptIN Story Slams, where a group gathers for a long afternoon, as individuals share testimonies of faith. We have had OptIN-led worship services, where all components of Sunday morning worship are led by OptIN participants.

> I didn't realize how naturally I default into theory or abstracted teaching until OptIN told me to stop and focus on the practices. It's getting easier, and it's paying off.
>
> **Pastor in Alabama**

OptIN is more than a curriculum; it's a methodology. This means the method of OptIN can be applied widely to differing situations.

The OptIN method is to equip participants with skills needed for Christian flourishing. This method can be applied to Sunday worship, and to Bible studies, and to youth groups, and to special church events.

It does not take the place of these already existing church events and programs, but it does seek to undergird them with Christian practices. We understand and value the need for churches to offer Bible studies and worship services and events, even youth groups or children's ministries. But, we also see a deficit in the lane of Christian practices and skill development. It is in this lane that OptIN operates.

Each unit includes a leader guidebook. These guides are meant to be as easy-to-follow as possible. With a small amount of preparation, a leader is set up to lead the group each week. In addition to the leader guidebook, there are companion resources for each of the units that are available for participants to use:

Where does Theology fit in?

When leading OptIN groups, the leader is encouraged to plug in their own theology. OptIN presents a sequence of activities aimed at concrete outcomes. We try to leave the teaching of ideas to each leader. For instance, in the Story Unit, the leader can share their ideas about the importance of storytelling and testimony with doctrine particular to their tradition.

Because OptIN focuses on *skills*, the only theology we do is practical.

Our theology claims that practicing the Christian life is centrally important. On that, we do not compromise. Our theology claims that we can better understand God and one another when we invest time into practicing the disciplines of faith. Any philosophy or doctrine is left open-ended so that different churches and individuals can use the program within their own theological context.

Other Units

Other units besides these three been developed and tested: Being Church looks at how to act as followers of Christ in our community and Exercising Leadership equips leaders within the church to lead with wisdom. Being Church is a unit that works well as a "new member" class within a church, or even as a "confirmation" curriculum for youth. Exercising Leadership is a unit that can be used as a part of already existing leadership meetings within a church. Instead of gathering a group together, this unit leverages the leadership board meetings of churches by *adding in* practical 15 minutes activities to equip people with the skills to lead well. The idea is to exercise leadership skills, whether for a few minutes before a meeting or at a designated retreat.

OptIN Kids

Our newest initiative is OptIN KIDS! It's been thrilling, not only because of the enthusiasm of children and the openness of their parents, but also because of how much we're learning. Plus, bright colors! (Tragically absent here but find them at optints.com)

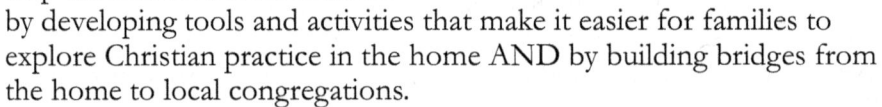

Our goal with OptIN Kids is to help families love their children by developing tools and activities that make it easier for families to explore Christian practice in the home AND by building bridges from the home to local congregations.

> *Every Bible Fun Card helped us talk about God's perspective... We could actually see the Biblical connection! It helped bring the stories to life*
>
> **Kid's Kit Parent Participant**

The foundation for faith development is the family, which means the place Christian practices are most important is also the family. To center the family, our tools and activities are packaged in a literal box and delivered to the home. Inside each box is an adventure with activities to explore one time-honored Christian practice (Story, Prayer, Worship), and tools that target anticipated obstacles.

Ideally, these boxes/kits are funneled through a local church, and include a leader guide offering simple and concrete ways these leaders can: check-in and encourage families, listen carefully to the needs of families, and plug those families back in tot he overall church life.

Dykstra states, "The faith of children is essential in the faith of the whole church. Indeed, adults can grow in the life of faith by participating with children in these practices, for the faith of children is a witness to us. Likewise, children grow in faith and in the life of faith as these practices become the fundamental habits of life around which their identity and character are formed."[35] With this in mind, OptIN Kids works to center practices so that children and adults can do the practices together.

Our first Kids Kit is the Story Investigators Kit. It is designed to help the family become investigators, looking for signs of God in the world around them. In this kit, there are 14 activities are aimed at two goals: 1)Uncovering stories of faith from the people who love you and 2)Telling faith stories of God's activity in your life.

These activities are scaffolded from simple to complex, as participants work through all the sub-skills needed to tell a story of God's activity: noticing God in the world, understanding God's stories in Scripture, linking our stories to Bible stories. As families work through the activities in the box, they are getting to know each other on a deeper level in the process. Parents and children are invited to do the activities together, so that parents can learn from their children, and children can learn from their parents.

> *The daily stories cards have helped my kids in finding God in their daily conversations... [My daugher] put an evidence tag on Dad, saying she sees God's protection in him. It was a very rewarding moment for him.*
> **Kid's Kit Parent Participant**

A Birthright That's Been Ignored

Dr. Lisa Miller builds a scientific case for developing the spiritual capacities of children. Parents work hard to

> *We have a more open communication about our faith with our children.*
> **Kid's Kit Parent Participant**

---

[35] Dykstra 2005, p. 45

equip children for good lives, but Miller claims "those conversations, elaborate schedules of extracurricular activities, and high aspirations often miss the single most crucial ingredient of all, the only thing science has shown to reliably predict fulfillment, success, and thriving: a child's spiritual development."[36] Miller rooted her claim in human nature: we are born with spirituality as a birthright, but this innate spiritual capacity must be cultivated or we will experience its lack and pursue inferior alternatives.[37] This means a fundamental goal of any program supporting faith transmission should be helping families rediscover Christian practices as necessary for children to flourish in life.

From Lecturers to Tour Guides

Americans no longer see religion as stewarding truths or the good life. Parents don't want their children indoctrinated by anyone—including the parent.[38] And yet, parents do think they should be doing more when it comes to spiritual formation.[39] They also tend to have relatively high levels of trust in their local congregation and pastor. This means there is a door open, not for didactic instruction, but for supporting exploration.

> *As a mom, I greatly appreciated having something other than me 'make us' do something like this. Because it was part of the activity box, my people just accepted that we had to do it—and we got a lot more participation even on the deeper activities.*
>
> **Kid's Kit Parent Participant**

Spirituality is important to many parents. But like eating healthier, the barriers are not about belief. The brilliance of services like Blue Apron is how they package readymade ingredients, simple instructions, and tailored recipes for a variety of diets. They make cooking good, healthy food easier. The same sort of intervention can help Christian parents explore Christian practices and pass them along to their children.

This shift in perspective is important because Americans look to congregations for support, not answers. The largest gap is not getting people into church; the gap is getting the practices of the church back

---

[36] Miller 2015, P. 24
[37] Ibid, 26
[38] Smith 2009, p. 177
[39] Nye 2009, p. 14

into the home. Church programs don't transmit religious belief to children. Parents do.

While we are not interested in removing church from its role in Christian formation, we are interested in pivoting slightly from being lecturers of right belief at church to being tour guides that guide families through spiritual practices. As tour guides, we can help families taste living water in the midst of a spiritually thirsty world.

> *My child seemed surprised about some of my answers... I think she realized some emotions I tend to hide from people, that just because I'm an adult doesn't mean I don't go through hard things too.*
> **Kid's Kit Parent Participant**

Starting Where We Agree

While our religious traditions are deep wells of wisdom for every aspect of life, there is a disconnect between the institutions that steward these resources and the families that need them. The gap is partially one of perception. These traditions are often treated as a repository of correct answers to a test. In contrast, religious parents believe they should, "equip their children with knowledge of their religion by routinely modeling its practices, values, and ethics, which children will then hopefully absorb and embrace for themselves."[40] Parents want to teach practices, not answers for a test.

This is where parents and churches can agree. We can centralize practices in order to transmit the faith to the next generation.

There is also significant research to suggest churches should prioritize the home because the family is the most fruitful ground for spiritual formation. Parents see themselves as primarily responsible for their children's faith formation. This is also functionally true. Parents (usually) have the trust and intimacy needed to build a spiritual foundation. By prioritizing the development of spiritual practices in the

> *I have noticed us actually sharing stories more than before... It brought about deep conversations of things we deal with often but don't talk about often.*
> **Kid's Kit Parent Participant**

---

[40] Smith and Adamczyk, 2021, p. 11

home, church leaders get to come alongside parents to undergird and support this important work.

Our next kit is focused on prayer, and specifically focused on daily prayer. Because prayer needs roots, and because families are stronger when they are rooted in God together. Our next kit is learning from the first, and the frequency with which we've heard parents sharing about their level of busyness, constant interruption, constant distraction, we've designed this intervention to be as small and easy as possible. Simple cards. Simple prayers. A daily rhythm that can fit into 60 seconds, or stretch for several minutes. The story of how we learned to pay this sort of close attention to people's lived experience is the story of the next chapter.

Chapter 5: Trade School Methods and Practices

There is a vast amount of scholarship and writing on the theory and practices of classroom education. There is a much smaller body of work on the theory and practices of teaching in a trade school. While there are significant overlaps around effective teaching for learning, there are differences. Clarity around outcomes is one of the most obvious. The trade school theorists in the book, *How to Teach Vocational Education,* observe that testing competence in an academic model is more challenging than a trade school. In a trade school, the test is: "Can you fillet the fish?"[41] That is, can you perform the task you are being equipped to perform? Trade schools produce concrete, visible outcomes.

Our work with OptIN has led us to research and study the pedagogy of a trade school, in order that we might use some of the insights to develop the program.

Introduction to The Trade School

It was the last day of our opening retreat for the OptIN Learning Community. A now familiar rhythm of inviting people to be guinea pigs had brought a fantastic group of pastors and denominational representatives from across the CP denomination to hear our pitch on Christian formation. During our retreat, we had visioned together, dialogued around the intersection of congregational renewal and discipleship, and brainstormed together. We had played innovation games, filled out post-its, and laughed. And, as is perhaps mandatory for such a gathering in the rural South, we had eaten copious amounts of delicious BBQ.

We were cleaning up the closing lunch with some volunteers from our church as the last guests drove away. Amid throwing trash away and distributing leftover food, our church volunteers asked how things had gone: *How did everyone respond?*

We shared that it was refreshing to hear from other church leaders that the church did need to adapt in order to thrive. Then we shared about our surprise: We had walked into this event ready to explain OptIN, with

---
[41] Lucas Et. al. 2012, sec. 3.3

an assiduously researched and rehearsed pitch built around a series of images for this new way of doing Christian formation. OptIN is like bumpers in a bowling alley, helping people develop rules of life for Christian flourishing. OptIN is like sports practice, where you build capacities for different parts of the Christian life. OptIN is like a set of rituals, where we work to build in habits of faith.

Unfortunately, our well-researched and rehearsed pitch wasn't landing with the group. They were politely suspicious, even confused. UNTIL, we landed on our final image: OptIN is like a trade school, where you develop the skills and learn the tools needed to follow Jesus.

For months, we had been circling around the shift from a traditional classroom model of Christian education focused on teaching and conceptual understanding to a model focused on equipping learners to perform tasks in the world. This meant practicing skills, getting familiar with tools, and whatever else trade schools did.

We had prayed that this group would help us discern where we needed to focus next. As we delivered this final explanatory image, the Spirit decided to take over our time together with a flashing neon sign: "Lean into the trade school idea."

As we shared our surprising insight, one of our church volunteers asked, "Would y'all want to visit the Jackson County trade school?"

"That would be awesome!"

"Let me call Jason," she said. Neither of us are from a small town, so we are still surprised by how tightly networked communities like Scottsboro can be. Our friend called Jason, who we discovered was her old friend Principal Davidson, the principal of the Earnest Pruett Trade and Career School.

Two days later, Principal Davidson was leading us on a tour of their facility.

The Spirit grabbed us again on this tour in the carpentry classroom. It was early in the semester, and the instructor was eager to explain his approach. He showed us a lesson book with technical drawings and explanations. Then he walked us to the back of the classroom, where a row of birdhouses stood against the wall. He said, "These are my students' first unit test."

The skills from their first unit were all utilized in designing the birdhouse: measuring and cutting the wood, attaching the wood, and then finishing it. Over the first few weeks, he had taught and the class had practiced each discreet skill. They were constantly learning and then testing their learning in hands-on application. All of this came together in this birdhouse project, which was a tangible indication of their growth, and where they still needed practice.

"All the skills they used to build that birdhouse are the skills we will keep using and building on to build furniture. They're the same skills and understandings they'll use to build a real house."

When we started OptIN, we did not intend to get into educational theory. We had been convicted by the growing literature around Christian practice, starting with Richard Foster's *Celebration of Discipline* and Dorothy Bass' *Practicing the Faith*.

We had preached on Christian practice, with sermon series focused on the elements of worship, on prayer, on service. This is not at all uncommon. Few would argue with an assertion that the Christian life should be put into practice. Being a Christian should affect how someone lives. Despite this, communicating the importance of practices, inspiring people about the power of practices, teaching on the necessity of the practices, did not consistently lead people deeper into daily rhythms of following Jesus. This finding is also not uncommon.

This carpentry class suggested a core part of why.

We believe the church today fails to adequately attend to what the incarnation means for how the church should approach learning and life change.

In our experience, the church will bypass practical matters of human nature—psychology, anthropology, behavioral change—because "the Holy Spirit" will handle the concrete and practical.

Church leaders know that behavior change is hard, even when people want to implement the change. Everyone knows the struggle of eating better, or exercising more, or reducing screen time. "This is the last time

I'm going to be so exhausted from work that I lose my temper with my kid." Right? We all know that's not actually how change happens. It's not enough to want change.

Church leaders and members know this, but church systems and practices don't. A church will invite people to make life changes—even substantial ones—at the end of a worship service with the expectation that concrete change might reasonably occur. Without accountability, or clarity on what practices are expected, or a clear plan on individual follow-up, how is this change going to happen? Still, church members and leaders will leave feeling like they *should* change, feeling like they *want* to change, and expecting themselves to come back next week living a substantively different life. Why?

Because of the Holy Spirit.

Anyone who does communication for a church knows we live in a hyper-saturated media environment where many people forget things almost as soon as they hear them. But preachers will speak on Sunday and trust people to carry the message with them and reflect all week. Why? *Because of the Holy Spirit.*

The Holy Spirit can and does exceed our human limits in pursuit of Gospel goals. There is scriptural justification for the Spirit's capacity to inspire and unleash rapid and profound change. So why isn't this experience more normative today?

A Willing Heart and Unskilled Hands

As the Body of Christ, the church must remember that the vehicle God chose for our redemption was not a disembodied spirit. It was a human being. Jesus was born with a body. Human beings have bodies. We are en-fleshed creatures. Jesus had a body. He had a family, and friends. He ate food and drank water and slept. He died. He was fully human (alongside his divinity). The perfection of Jesus in the flesh did not transform him into a superman.

> *Whether it's tea ceremony, karate, or calligraphy, you follow a form until it becomes second nature. That's how spiritual disciplines work—you pray, read Scripture, fast, worship—not to check boxes, but because over time, these practices form you.*
>
> **Pastor in Kentucky**

His perfection submitted his humanity to the work of the Spirit and the will of the Father.

When the church looks to the Holy Spirit to supersede our human nature so we might immediately arrive at a life of faithfulness, we forget that the faithfulness of Jesus was lived out in him being human faithfully. When the Holy Spirit comes to transform us into the image of Jesus, this is less a work of overriding our human nature and more reshaping our human nature into its proper form. There are new ways of doing things as a follower of Christ, not just new ways of thinking. New thought comes from new ideas and new ways of doing come through practice and skill development.

An important insight from our revelation in that carpentry classroom was that the church needs to pay closer attention to the embodied experience of Christians trying to be Christian. It cannot be a church's responsibility to give congregants good ideas for living as Christians, and then leave the rest of the responsibility of actual change to them to figure out on their own. Some do figure out the disciplines of faith, but many do not. Too often, the end result is that the heart is willing, but the hands and feet have no skills to carry out that willingness.

Christian teaching on practice can easily go something like this (we are writing confessionally from experience): "Here is why [Christian practice] is important. Here are a variety of ways it has been historically performed. Here are some exemplars who did that practice very well, and how it impacted the world around them."

Translating this approach into a different context makes the problem more obvious. Picture a teacher stands up in front of her carpentry class and begins to explain that we have an incredible housing shortage. She presents statistics on the shortage and its impact on housing prices. Then she explains the impact houses have on families' lives. She talks about the satisfying career that her students could have if they build houses for a living. Then she concludes with a slideshow of beautiful houses that successful carpenters have built.

If the teacher presented well, these students leave convinced that building houses is important work. They leave inspired by the beautiful houses they've seen. They believe that building houses is a sustainable career choice.

None of which addresses the basic question: are these students any more equipped to build a house than they were before? Obviously not. And yet, it is our experience that churches routinely treat conviction, inspiration, and belief as sufficient to produce change in congregants. It is routine for churches to approach teaching practice as though it is an idea.

Standing in that carpentry classroom, as the teacher shared about his curriculum and methods, we realized we had been making a series of well-meaning mistakes. More than anything, we had been "teaching" Christian practices by explaining why they were needed. Even when we practiced a particular skill, it was a short, one-time-only practice. More often, we would model what a particular practice looks like. This sort of modeling is an important first step in learning a skill, but it is only a first step. What we had not been doing was teaching skills, dedicating time to practicing them, and sequencing a progression according to complexity.

This satirical image is used by entrepreneur Seth Godin to make the same point. Imitating how skills are often taught, the instructions begin helpfully with, "Draw two circles." In Fig 2., the instructions accurately model the end product of drawing an owl. Unless someone already knows how to draw, these instructions are totally useless in helping them progress from the two circles to the finished project.

What's worse, the instructions imply, "If you can't progress from Fig 1. to Fig 2., that's your fault." Not only does it fail to equip the user. It implies failure is the users fault.

How to draw an Owl.

"A fun and creative guide for beginners"

Fig 1. Draw two circles

Fig 2. Draw the rest of the owl

Apocalyptic Unmasking

The word "apocalypse" means something like exposing or laying bare. It unmasks a situation. That moment in the Earnest Pruett Trade and Vocational School, as the Holy Spirit confronted us with that row of student birdhouses, was apocalyptic. It unmasked something in the task God had given us.

We had not been equipping our congregants to perform the tasks we were expecting them to do. Like the meme above, we might teach them to draw two circles and gesture toward the end goal. Moments in a class or worship would effectively model the first steps of a particular Christian practice. Preaching and teaching might clarify the importance, or the beauty, or the joy, of that end goal.

> *Working through the Exercising Leadership cards in a Session meeting, I was shocked at how many of my elders had never considered that they were 'called' into leadership... The cards made them pay consider it. Seeing them name their gifts to one another was deeply encouraging.*
> **Pastor in Alabama**

Then we were leaving it to the congregant to bridge that impossible gap.

When earnest and honest Christians experience failure in trying to follow Jesus—when their prayer life falls short, when they don't see God at work in their stories, when worship feels empty—whose fault is that?

If these practices are a matter of conviction or belief, then the failure might be the failure of each individual believer. It is something insufficient in their heart. They need to try harder and believe more. Plenty of Christians carry precisely this guilt. Often enough, we have carried this guilt: "The reason I'm not hearing God's voice, the reason worship is suddenly stale, is because I don't love God enough."

> *Before OptIN, I was honestly feeling pretty burned out. Just discouraged about what I was accomplishing. Seeing transformation in people's lives has been renewing for me as a pastor and for my church.*
> **Pastor in Alabama**

Or, it could be the fault of the preacher. The preacher should have delivered a sufficiently inspirational or convicting message to elevate the faith lives of their congregation. Plenty of preachers carry this burden. Looking at an earnest and faithful flock, feeling the responsibility of inspiring change and watching their congregation stay remarkably the same. If they were more excellent, more like the megachurch pastors who keynote conferences and fill stadiums, then their congregation would be experiencing deeper life in Christ.

The first of these explanations misunderstand our human nature, and so loads individuals with inhuman expectations.

The second of these displaces the slow work of transformation by the Holy Spirit with a fast work of being overwhelmed and inspired by a pastor's charisma.

Behind these failures is a different root problem. The gap between drawing two circles and drawing an owl is a gap of skill development. Someone attempting to bridge this gap without more help will be experienced as failure. After being invited time after time to experience the depth and transformative power of Christian practices and experiencing failure and frustration, people stop believing that the Christian practices work.

Treating Christian practices as metaphorical "birdhouses," has helped us reclaim the incarnational nature of these practices. As that carpentry teacher talked about his students developing muscles, we asked, "Are there muscles that we need to exercise to pray better?"

For instance, to pray effectively, someone must be able to pay attention long enough to settle into God's presence. Or someone needs to be able to sit in silence to hear God. Or someone needs to know how to hear God's Word through Scripture. All of these are muscles we need to build in order to pray.

It has helped us attend to the difference between having people attend worship and preparing them to participate in worship. It has helped us recognize that church history is full of tools, practices, and exercises meant to help earnest and faithful believers confronting challenging circumstances.

This revelatory moment was so important to us that we have used the image of a birdhouse as our logo.

Vocational Pedagogy

Pedagogy may be an unfamiliar word for people who are not educators. But the Greek word "pedagogy" means "methods and practices of teaching." All teachers study pedagogy as part of their career preparation. But coaches and bosses have pedagogies, theories for how their people will learn to do what they need them to do.

OptIN's focus on Christian practice goes beyond the mere importance of having an active faith. A trade school should not merely be concerned with communicating the importance of a trade or getting students to try a trade. Instead, a trade school is concerned with developing competence. In studies of trade school methodology, this is called a clear line of sight.[42]

> A clear line of sight to work is critical because vocational learners must be able to see why they are learning what they are learning, understand what the development of occupational expertise is all about, and experience the job in its context. The real work context should inform the practice of vocational teaching and learning for learners, teachers and trainers.[43]

Approaching practice as a trade school means understanding the real-world context in which Christians are trying to live and then building a curriculum that equips them to live faithfully in that context. Participants should understand the desired impact of what they're learning on their lives outside of the practice space.

At a trade school, theoretical understanding is still important, but it is not success. Success is if students are able to competently perform their trade in the world. For the trade school, if a student graduated and started a business or took a job doing a task that they were not able to do competently, that would be a failure. The reason is fairly obvious. Despite their short-term success—getting the job or starting the business—it will quickly become evident that this student can't perform at the necessary

---

[42] This study identifies a clear line of sight to work as one of their four keys to adult vocational school. The four keys are "1). a clear line of sight to work on all vocational programmers; 2. 'dual professional' teachers and trainers who combine occupational and pedagogical expertise, and are trusted and given the time to develop partnerships and curricula with employers; 3. access to industry-standard facilities and resources reflecting the ways in which technology is transforming work; 4. clear escalators to higher level vocational learning, developing and combining deep knowledge and skills."[42] It's About Learning: Excellent adult vocational teaching and learning. p. 14.

[43] Ibid., p. 14.

level. They will lose their job, or will need remedial training to be brought up to the proper skill-level.

For this reason, trade schools depend on open lines of communication with the trades they serve. Trade schools like to recruit teachers from the profession itself, helping to bridge that gap between the classroom and the "real world" within their instructor.

What happens if churches send Christians out into the world who are not equipped to live as Christians in the world? What happens when churches expect people to pray who have not been equipped to pray?

Dallas Willard reflects on how the tradition he grew up in emphasized scripture reading and prayer, as well as worship, but "I was not given to understand that these had to be practiced in a certain way if they were to make a real difference in one's life."[44] That is, the tradition he grew up in assumed that prayer, scripture and worship worked automatically.

The problem with this assumption, for Willard, is that he discovers it is possible to perform Christian practices in a way that they will not make a real difference. The importance of practice does not mean that practices automatically work. Instead, the importance means we need to pay attention to how they work.

There is a visceral resistance to this insight in the church. We feel it, too. Saying to someone, "You are praying wrong," feels elitist. Who are any of us to step into the middle of someone else's faith and tell them how to pray?

> *I want to cherish the good traditions of the church while balancing tradition with freedom. We need the Holy Spirit's guidance to bring new life into practices that risk becoming empty formalism.*
>
> **Pastor in Kentucky**

But if Willard is right, if it is possible to perform Christian practices in a way where they will not make a real difference in someone's life, then we have to have conversations about how practices work and how they don't. Otherwise, there will be people who are convinced that prayer doesn't work, because they tried praying and it didn't work. There will be people who don't think scripture is inspired because they tried reading it

---

[44] Willard 2014, p. 390

and they weren't inspired. In our experience, both of these realities not only exist but are common.

Christian Practices Suffer from the Fall

Lauren Winner begins her helpfully uncomfortable book, The Danger of Christian Practice, with the reminder that, "Nothing, not even the good practices of the church, is untouched by the Fall."[45] While God remains perfect, our conversation with God (prayer) is not perfect. Our performance of divine tasks (service, worship, scripture) is touched by our own fallen hearts and minds and institutions.

In her survey of the explosion of literature and emphasis, Winner is concerned that "Many current discussions of Christian practices are too rosy—are pristinated—and fail to acknowledge, let alone account for or respond to, the sin entailed by those practices."[46] In the discussion cited above, Willard goes on to emphasize the intensity and focus in attention with the conversely slowed pace of life necessary to pray or read scripture effectively. If prayer and scripture unfold slowly, then Christians need to slow our lives down enough to let prayer and scripture work. As embodied creatures, humans cannot choose to be unaffected by chaotic schedules and distracted mental states because prayer and scripture are important.

Winner's question pushes deeper than this. She posits that certain Christian practices are inherently disposed to certain types of sinfulness because of the Fall. Her goal isn't to diminish the importance of Christian practices. Instead, she wants to make sure we don't approach them with a naïve optimism. "Identification, rather than obfuscation, of the damage characteristic of indispensable Christian practices helps us describe the practices more truthfully, and helps us be on the alert for deformations."[47]

Through our experimentation with OptIN, we have come to agree with Winner's claim. There is an under-recognized mismatch between what people can do and what churches assume they can do. This is fueled by a naïve optimism about how Christian practice works, and what is necessary to engage in practices well. Church systems make assumptions

---

[45] Winner 2018, p. 1
[46] Ibid., p. 167
[47] Winner 2018, p. 17

about the people who participate in them. In general, churches assume that praying well, and praying as a Christian, is easy enough to do without assistance or formal training. They assume that prayer doesn't depend on any prerequisite understandings or abilities. Church systems assume this because they do not provide assistance, formal training, or practice meant to develop foundational capacities.

Any church that invites members to, "Go home and open the Bible," has a system that assumes their members have everything they need to read the Bible well.

> I didn't anticipate how horrible people are horrible at taking directions. I said several times these stories should be 5 minutes... one participant's story lasted seventeen minutes. Another lasted thirty five. The shame is, being too long made their stories confusing. The audience lost focus. It covered up the beauty underneath.
>
> **Pastor in Kentucky**

Churches assume congregants can recognize and narrate God's activity in their lives—even amidst all the other stories and pressures and distractions swirling around—whenever they don't have time set aside to support noticing God and sharing what God is doing.

Many churches assume that "worship," is a self-evident activity, something people are inherently familiar with and able to do, and something that doesn't require practice, training, or explanation to do well.

This is precisely the sort of "pristinated" practice that Winner is drawing our attention toward. When church systems invite members into Christian practices without training, without sustained attention on how these practices are being embodied, without a recognition of how these practices can go wrong or what cultural practices might be influencing them, churches are assuming they will automatically work.

We fell into this trap. We assumed that if we could convince our members to pray more, or read the Bible more, or come to church more, that would automatically be effective. Our job was to inspire, to invite, to convince our members that the practices were important. Embodying the practices was a personal responsibility, not a systemic one, and embodying the practices well would flow naturally from our congregant's desire to embody them. This wasn't true.

It is crucial for the church to identify such assumptions in our systems and schedules. To better understand the point, compare the church to other sorts of places and activities.

A sports team will not assume athletes can show up and participate. Being on a sports team assumes a certain hierarchical structure—the coach is in charge and the team follows her authority. Sports also require skills and understanding. It assumes certain commitments around participation in practice, treatment of teammates, effort in games.

If someone can't dribble or shoot, they will struggle in basketball. If they don't know the rules of basketball, they will struggle. If they aren't physically in shape, they will struggle. Skills, knowledge, and fitness will all impede someone's ability to fully participate. When someone joins a sports team, they either meet these criteria or there is an assumption that they are joining the team with the intention of practicing and developing those skills, understandings, and level of fitness until they do.

It is important that this isn't just sports being exclusive. A coach who doesn't have a primary goal of "winning" should still have these expectations because these criteria affect participation. Imagine if a coach put a player lacking the skills, understandings, and fitness into a game, and told them, "All that matters is you try your best." Imagine that player's experience.

Trying to dribble and losing the ball. Missing shots. Trying harder at tasks that don't depend on effort, they depend on skill. Imagine the frustration and discouragement. Getting called for penalties they didn't realize they were committing because they didn't know the rules. Trying to run and their lungs are burning because they weren't prepared. While it is obviously the individual that isn't prepared, this is more the coach's fault for putting them into a situation with no preparation.

It is our contention that church participation is more like being a member of a gym, not a sports team. The YMCA has certain rules and policies, but once you walk in, the gym doesn't tell participants what to do or where to go. It doesn't require a level of skill, understanding or fitness. People choose to attend, and the gym provides the facilities, the equipment, maybe classes or access to pick-up games of basketball.

Significantly, the gym also doesn't take responsibility for people's growth or experience. If you want to join a gym and never increase in fitness, that's ok. There is no group activity or game where your skills are important. If you want to join the gym and never attend, that's ok. There aren't people at the gym who rely on you. Unfortunately, church falls into the same category as being a gym member, but it should function more like a sports team. Part of the difference between a gym and sports team is a sports team has a shared objective and a collective identity.

If Christian practices are embodied behaviors that, therefore, depend on certain skills, understandings, and capabilities, then by expecting congregants to participate in practices without teaching and equipping them, the church is setting them up for experiences of failure and frustration. When church systems are built around mistaken assumptions about Christian practices, the practitioners are not equipped to do what they are expected to do. They are not equipped to do what they expect themselves to be able to do. The church is setting them up to experience these practices as things that don't work.

In our early experiments with OptIN, we invited participants on a 10-month sprint through the practices. As an example, the groups spent about a month on prayer practices. It wasn't built around lectures or readings. Participants were exposed to the importance of silence, experienced the power of liturgy and unscripted prayer, and tried different prayer practices and tools like a buffet or a tasting menu. Without a doubt, the Spirit did move. People were impacted.

The group's positive response masked the pedagogy's lack of efficacy. Participants quickly recognized that silence was hard but necessary for prayer. They quickly realized particular tools would be powerful in particular life-situations. With a glimpse of the depth their prayer lives could have, they all intended to lean into all these insights.

In assessing their progress months later, it was discouraging for us—and for them—to realize how little had come from this newly discovered potential. The process helped them realize there was a gap between their existing prayer lives and what their prayer lives could be. It helped them recognize the complexity of praying well in different situations. It had not equipped them to close that gap.

Our curriculum had recognized that our faith is embodied, and it had centered embodied teaching by exploring Christian practices together. It still had not taken seriously enough what it means that we are embodied creatures. The curriculum still assumed that once participants understood that the faith needs to be embodied, and saw what that could look like, things would naturally improve. It still failed to understand the church's role in helping members embody the faith.

The Trade School Pyramid

Bill Lucas, Ellen Spencer and Guy Claxton, wrote a book called *How to Teach Vocational Education: A Theory of Vocational Pedagogy* (2012, sec. 3.2). They explain that vocational education has three corners, like a pyramid.

- One corner of the pyramid is *materials*. A plumber, carpenter, electrician, or hairdresser learn to use tools and materials within the trade. It involves learning skills by trial-and-error. Through trial-and-error, these tradespeople learn concrete skills by repetition, solving problems, and making adjustments.
- The other corner of vocational education deals with *people*. A child-care provider, a medical technician, a massage therapist, a chef learns skills by interacting with people and adapting as necessary. This area involves learning skills, conversations, responding to the needs and desires of the client, and adapting to each situation.
- The third corner of the pyramid is what Lucas et. al. calls *symbols*. Accountants, computer programmers, or graphic designers works with abstract concepts, or symbols. These people develop skills related to critical thinking so they can produces outputs that provide information.

While there are three separate corners of this pyramid, vocations usually have overlap. They are not neatly boxed into their corner. A hairdresser deals with materials (chemicals, tools, machines) and with people. A plumber deals with materials and symbols (building codes).

OptIN leans into the *materials* and *people* corners of vocational pedagogy. Through OptIN, Christian formation is grounded in hands-on skill development, using tools and materials that can help in the endeavor. And OptIN leans on family units and small groups for conversations with people, responding and adapting to particular situations. Christian practices should be in a reciprocal dialogue with practitioners about the challenges they face, where things are working, and needs they have.

Our claim, and the basis of the OptIN approach to Christian formation is that the things *we do* in church are skills we can learn: prayer, telling testimonies, worship. Without learning to do these skills well, we will be resigned to doing them poorly. Which means in order to be a good carpenter, or a good hairdresser, or an effective person who prays, one needs to learn hands-on-skills.

Chapter 6: What We Learned about Learning

The following subsections describe what we learned about learning: the theory of change, sequencing skills from simple to complex, using the right tools, having specific objectives and outcomes, and keeping it engaging. There could be a lot more here, especially drawing from the growing science of learning and practice, but we want to at least gesture toward some relevant insights for church leaders.

The Theory of Change

Part of why Christians have impoverished experiences of church is because they have not been equipped to fully participate in church. Likely, they have been invited into what churches do, but not equipped with the skills to actually participate.

This gets at the fact that the church needs to develop a better "Theory of Change." A theory of change is a working understanding of how exactly a particular change is going to take place. The church's default theory of change is what we call the "New Year's Resolution (with Jesus)" model of change. By January 1st of each year, countless individuals decide they are going to exercise regularly. Every gym is flooded with people. But by mid-February, the crowds have died down, and with the exception of a few new faces, the gym's 'old-timers' are the only ones regularly working out.

A New Year's resolution is undergirded by inspiration and motivation. But inspiration and motivation only instigate life-change; On their own, they are limited. Human beings need more than inspiration to support behavioral change. Zeal and motivation are a great starting point, but they will not get you to the finish line. Ask any runner! They know it takes months of practice and conditioning, in addition to motivation, to get to the finish line.

In church, we motivate and inspire toward life change week after week, in preaching and teaching. We inspire people to want to read Scripture more, to want to attend worship more regularly, to want to serve their neighbor. But inspiration, on its own, is limited. It's not that inspiration is not needed. It is. But inspiration/motivation is only *one* of the *three* components needed for behavior change.

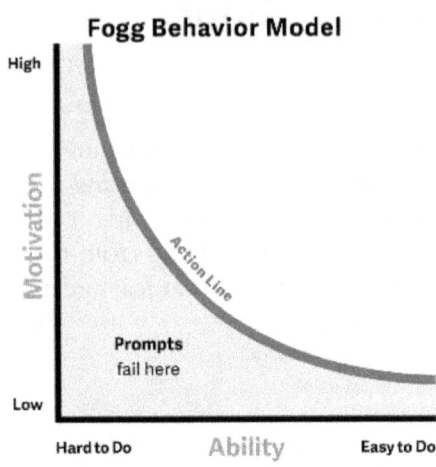

Dr. BJ Fogg identifies three key components necessary for behavioral change: motivation, ability, and prompt. "Any solution designed to change behaviours must orchestrate all three elements - Motivation, Ability, Trigger - coming together at one moment. The common mistake is to focus solely on motivation. But the path to success often is about increasing ability and triggering [prompting] the behaviour."[48]

Fogg's model should lead the church to pay attention to why Christian practices fail. This sort of attention means paying attention to the practice in people's daily lives. Motivation naturally fluctuates, according to the time of day and context. People might feel motivated to pray in church, or in the face of a tragedy, or at small group. Motivation will be different at work or after an exhausting day or in the middle of fun with kids. The obvious importance of motivation is why it presents as the most significant of the three, and as Fogg notes above, the "most common mistake is to focus solely on motivation."

The other two essential elements of behavior are ability and prompt. Motivation and ability are in a compensatory relationship with each other. When extremely motivated, people can accomplish even hard-to-do tasks. When a task is extremely easy, it can be accomplished with even low motivation. But Fogg invites us beyond motivation.

When it comes to supporting a behavior or practice, Fogg first looks to increasing ability. He sequences increasing ability by first recommending training for the skill, then deploying a tool, and finally shrinking the skill to something more initially achievable.

Part of our work with OptIN has been breaking down disciplines into skills and abilities that can be practiced. Prayer is undergirded by abilities of silence, attention, familiarity with God's presence, knowledge of historic prayer, purity of heart. These abilities affect the depth of

---

[48] Fogg 2021, p. 26.

people's experience in prayer. Prayer is enhanced by practicing these skills. The stronger the skills, the easier it is.

The final part of this behavior trifecta is a prompt. There can be motivation and ability in abundance, but without a prompt, the behavior will not take place. A calendar or a to-do list is a prompt. A schedule is a prompt. When my tooth hurts, I am prompted to go to the dentist and get it checked. Likewise, moving the healthy food to the front of the pantry so it is seen first is a prompt. Putting running shoes beside the bed so you wake up and see them is a prompt. Fogg also calls these "triggers," and identifies three different categories of triggers suited to different sorts of situations.

The first sort is a spark. "When a person lacks motivation to perform a target behavior, a trigger should be designed in tandem with a motivational element. I call this type of trigger a "spark." Examples of sparks can range from text that highlights fear to videos that inspire "hope."[49] These are triggers that remind someone about an action, and include motivation built in. Churches use behavioral sparks when they send a social media post with a compelling image and an invitation to pray. The prompt to pray is sent with the motivation.

The second sort of prompt is "for users that have high motivation but lack ability,"[50] and Fogg calls it a facilitator. "The goal of a facilitator is to trigger the behavior while also making the behavior easier to do."[51] This is the overall function of an OptIN group. Participation assumes a level of motivation and a desire to change. When the group is gathered together, participants do the hard work of experimenting and developing ability. The OptIN group facilitates behavior change.

Fogg's third sort of prompt is a signal. "This… type works best when people have both the ability and the motivation to perform the target behavior. The signal doesn't seek to motivate people or simplify the task. It just serves as a reminder… An ordinary example of a signal is a traffic light that turns red or green. The traffic light is not trying to motivate me.; it simply indicates when a behavior is appropriate." OptIN has created tools that function as signals: prayer flip books that serve as a reminder to pray. Story cards that remind congregants to share stories of

---

[49] Ibid., p. 24.
[50] Ibid., p. 24.
[51] Ibid., p. 25.

God's activity. And worship guides showing the elements of worship and ways to apply them to our daily lives.

By closely attending to congregant's lived situations, the church can begin to see where practices break down. Is it a failure of motivation? Is it a failure of ability? Or is it just that people needed a reminder? This affects the sorts of prompts that are appropriate to deploy in response.

If the church is to take seriously the work of helping our members live new lives in light of Jesus, we must attend to these sorts of details. It is not enough to gesture to the Spirit. It's not that the Spirit can't override the limit of these abilities, or provide a burst of motivation, or a miraculous prompt in the form of a nudge. The Spirit can. But normally, the Spirit works within the bounds of our humanity.

Fogg's research has led him to the "Tiny Habits" approach. "Make the behavior so tiny that you don't need much motivation."[52] By focusing on tiny habits, "you don't need to rely on the unreliable nature of motivation." The church often invites people into a behavioral change that is far too big to implement: "Pray more" is not a concrete or small shift. A better invitation would be: "Pray this short and scripted prayer (that I have provided for you), everyday this week." Then we will try forming and expressing our own prayers using different outlines.

It is not enough to choose any small behavior, however. Because motivation is necessary, even a small inconvenience won't happen without desire. Fogg emphasizes that it is best to "help people do what they already want to do." The church can and should support new behaviors by having a clear line of sight between the practice and its importance for living well with Jesus. Our experience as pastors was that many followers of Christ are motivated, but they lack skills. And yet, we, as pastors, still continue to preach and teach in hopes that congregants are more motivated to solve the 'skill' problem on their own.

Finally, Fogg notes the benefit of changing with a group. Changing alone is hardest because the inertia of our relationships pulls us back toward how we were living. This is one reason whole family units are an OptIN priority whenever it's possible. Experimenting together also allows a group to learn from each other, give each other advice, share tools, and

---

[52] Fogg 2021, p. 27.

learn from each other's mistakes. It provides energy and accountability that keep people going when things get hard.

A common discipline in our project is to think about Christian practices through the lens of less spiritual activities. So, let us just say, we have yet to meet anyone who was taught to drive by learning the intricacies of an internal combustion engine. Nor would we trust that someone knew how to drive because, "They really, *really* wanted to."

In normal life, we don't assume a connection between how badly someone wants to do something and how well they are able to perform the task. And yet, this is what the New Year's Resolution Theory of Change Assumes.

Or, we assume that the theory will translate directly into practice. The ins-and-outs, the pitfalls and the opportunities are assiduously detailed. Only after a thorough examination of prayer or story or worship is the individual invited to participate in those practices. The participant is "freed" to decide how to practice on their own, or they are "burdened," with having to invent the practice for themselves, applying all that theory admist the complexities of their context. And doing it without the help of the teacher or community. In church, we love teaching the intricacies of an internal combustion engine, instead of teaching people how to drive.

Someone learns to drive with another experienced driver in the car. This usually takes place on a quiet street or in an empty parking lot. We don't take our 15-year-olds onto the freeway or out in the middle of rush hour the first time they sit behind the steering wheel.

But Christians are expected to drive with no practice. They are routinely thrown into spiritual practices in the middle of life. We expect followers of Christ to pray or to tell their story of faith in the middle of a critical situation, or with their kid yelling, or in the face of serious doubts. This is like learning to drive on the freeway.

OptIN's lane is to support the practice of spiritual disciplines. We do the theory, but we want to embed those insights in our pedagogy, not expect participants to design their own pedagogical framework. Theoretical rabbit holes are too tempting as escapes.

Learning about praying is a lot like learning about exercising. It's easier. It's interesting. It even gives the learner a sense of progress. But it's not actually exercise. Likewise, watching someone authentically worship is a lot like watching someone eat. It's moving. Inspirational. But the observer isn't spiritually filled and renewed unless it leads them into their own authentic encounter with God.

Studying an activity, or discussing an activity is not necessarily connected to doing that activity. It's easier and less embarrassing to engage the practice in the abstract than to try to embody it. Which means that retreating into the theoretical is a temptation leading away from embodied practice. This consistently surfaces in OptIN groups. Talking about the importance of silence is easier than experiencing the discomfort that comes as five minutes turns into six, and the participant can't tell if that's God talking or their impatience. That experience of silence is mentally exhausting. Naming what you think God was saying is potentially embarrassing. It is easier, for the leader and the participants, to retreat into the safer space of abstraction.

In response to this temptation, OptIN resources have cut back on abstracted discussion questions. Instead of learning goals like "Students will understand that their stories are influenced by God's story," an OptIN unit has a goal more like, "Students will attempt to reframe several personal stories from their life by using the Biblical story." The theoretical still matters. It is assumed and embedded in the concrete learning goal. But the theory is hidden. Participants don't need all the theory to get the benefit of the practice. With this approach, we are trying to minimize the temptation to retreat into the abstract by supporting sustained effort and experimentation in Christian practices.

Another way to approach this conversation is the language of a theory of a change. A theory of change is a provisional explanation for how a set of actions, activities, and strategies will lead to a particular outcome. Behind OptIN is a concern that many churches have an assumed theory of change that is not actually generating change.

The theory of change OptIN is investigating is relatively simple; Christians must be equipped to participate in the life of the church and private practices of the faith. This work of equipping for participation is foundational, and often neglected. In order for congregations to thrive, congregants must have the skills and understandings necessary to be faithful participants in the life of the church. Absent this ability, we would expect to see church work increasingly centralized among "professionals," especially pastors and worship leaders. We would expect lay people to routinely experience anemic Christian practices that aren't sufficient for the challenges and opportunities of their life. Because their ability with Christian practices is not sufficient, they will lean on more familiar and practiced secular skills. Yoga and meditation replace prayer. Bridge club replaces corporate worship. Netflix replaces the telling and hearing of Christian stories.

Because Christians we meet generally want to follow Jesus, we don't believe the primary barrier to congregational thriving is one of inspiration. Instead, we believe the failure is systemic. It is methodological. Churches are operating with a deficient theory of change. As discussed above, church systems are built on faulty assumptions. Many churches accidentally expect their members to invent a Christian way of life. Many churches accidentally assume their congregants can identify their sins to confess, truthfully narrate God's activity in their life, love people they don't like, and a host of other profoundly complex and challenging tasks. Or, church systems assume that practicing and preparing for these sorts of tasks is something for individual Christians to do on their own. But this fundamentally misunderstands how lives change and how learning takes place. This individualizes the Christian life precisely where individuals most need the support of the historic tradition and expert practitioners of the faith.

Our theory of change centers on increasing conviction and belief by supporting deeper experiences of the Christian life. We want to support congregational flourishing by better equipping individual members to faithfully participate in the life of the church. As a sequence, it would look like this:

1. Gather church members and practice the skills necessary for participating in the life of faith;
2. Support low-stakes experimentation with Christian practices together, so that;
3. Individuals and the congregation are more deeply planted in the fruitful soil of the Christian life, and become able to bear more fruit (to their joy and the flourishing of their community).

A Sequence of Skills: Simple to Complex

On our tour of the vocational school in town, we peeked into an electrician's classroom. There was still a chalkboard at the front of the class, and rows of tables like a chemistry classroom. But the whole back of the classroom consisted of different combinations of walls with wires running through it, poking out in multicolored clumps. Different types of motors had metal plates cut off to show the wiring inside. All of this was laid out and organized so that a concept could be taught in theory and immediately put into practice.

There were different mock walls set up with different kinds of wiring. They were sequenced from simple to complex, which was obvious by looking at the different walls and seeing the growing complexity of wires, electrical boxes, switches, fuses, and electrical appliances. As students learn electrical skills, they begin with the easiest wall of wiring and work toward the most complicated.

John Thompson, in his book, *Foundations of Vocational Education*, explains the *Allen Method* of designing curriculums for different trades taught in vocational schools.[53] The *Allen Method* involves observing the trade and then designing the training instructions around that analysis. Similar skills are blocked into a group to be taught together, and the skills are sequenced in order of learning difficulty to reach mastery of the trade.

OptIN is not a curriculum; it is a methodology like the *Allen Method*. OptIN breaks down spiritual disciplines into actionable activities, sequencing activities from easy to hard.

Donnella (Dana) Meadows, in her book, *Thinking in Systems*[54] tells the story of two watch makers. Both produce quality watches, but one is better than the other. Any time a watchmaker is interrupted, he or she has to start the entire assembly from the beginning. One of the watchmakers came up with a solution to interruptions by making subassemblies; this watchmaker would build separate sections of the watch, and then put them all together at the very end. This change in the process increased production. The slow watch maker built the entire watch at one time, So interruptions resulted in starting all over. By breaking down the process into smaller steps, one watchmaker was more effective.

---

[53] Thompson 1973, pp. 166–67
[54] Meadows, 2008

OptIN is a methodology that breaks Christian disciplines down into subunits with two levels of subassembly. On the one hand each spiritual discipline involves a series of steps, or activities, that leads to a new capacity. Secondly, instead of trying to produce a whole Christian all at once, OptIN frames spirituality as different Christian disciplines. For example: let's build our story, lets practice prayer, let's rehearse worship. Each separate unit is part of building a wholistic spirituality. We believe that these two levels of subassembly allow practitioners of the faith to be more effective.

Using the Right Tools

Back to our tour of the Jackson County trade school, we were led to a classroom where a career mechanic had retired from his shop to teach another generation. We walked in as he laid out a bucket of different of wrenches. "You need to know what each of these are, or you'll make your life a lot harder for yourself," he explained, waving at our guide as we passed through.

Having the correct wrench is important for a mechanic. They all do different things.

No carpenter feels incompetent because they can't pound a nail in with their fist (no tool), or with a screwdriver (wrong tool). The carpenter knows that he needs a hammer for a nail and a screwdriver for a screw.

But the contemporary church, by default, expects Christians to pray effectively from their own heart, or to tell a compelling faith story without guidance, and to jump into worship without any rehearsal or scaffolding. In the church, we over-rely on willpower and desire. We forget about tools.

> *I used to use scripture to pray a lot, but I'd fallen out of the habit. Leading the prayer unit got me back into even more deeply. It's amazing the way God can speak to you, boom!, through a book that's been around for two thousand years.*
>
> **Pastor in Alabama**

Having the correct tools to help with spiritual disciplines is important to a healthy spiritual life.

Prayer, as a practice, has a long history of tools: lectio divina, examen prayer, imaginative prayer, praying the Psalms, and so many more. The

Bible is full of stories of faith: ones of triumph and ones of defeat, ones of grief and others of joy, stories of healing and stories of heartache. To tell compelling stories of faith, we should recognize the Word of God as a helpful guide for putting our own stories into words.

There are countless different kinds of wrenches, and they all are useful tools for different tasks. Through routine practice with the different tools available, a mechanic can reach mastery in their trade. OptIN works to provide or develop tools to help with putting the spiritual disciplines into practice.

Specific Objectives and Concrete Standards

In that carpentry class, it was helpful that there was a concrete outcome at the end of their first unit: a birdhouse. Students saw the teacher's already completed birdhouse before they began to construct their own. They had a clear picture of where they were headed when that first unit of carpentry began.

In Daniel Coyle's, *The Little Book of Talent,* he affirms that "Every skill is built out of smaller pieces – what scientist call chunks. Chunks are to skills what letters of the alphabet are to language. Alone, each is nearly useless, but when combined into bigger chunks … they can build something complex and beautiful."[55] In the parlance of carpentry, measuring, nailing, sawing, design, are pieces one must accomplish to build a birdhouse. Coyle then explains, "… No matter what skill you set out to learn, the pattern is always the same: See the whole thing. Break it down to its simplest elements. Put it back together. Repeat".[56] As Coyle describes, skill development involves practice, mistakes, correction.[57] Anders Ericsson, a phycologist and professor, explains success is the result of trying new things, with a process that leads to clear goals (objectives).[58] For both Coyle and Ericsson, learning skills needs a stated end goal, that is, an objective.

At the start of every OptIN unit, participants know the desired outcome. We want them to be able to see the birdhouse at the outset of the class.

---

[55] Coyle 2012, p. 45
[56] Ibid., p. 46
[57] Ibid., p. 26
[58] Ericsson 2016, p. 22

For example, in the "Building Stories" unit, the final result is that every person in the class will tell a story of God's activity in his or her life to the group. The rest of the unit is a constellation of practices that support that result: recognizing God's activity in life, practicing storytelling, connecting our stories to stories in Scripture. The desired outcome is explicitly named, and then intentionally supported.

OptIN recognizes that most local churches are not invested in developing objectives and standards related to Christian formation, at least not related to *skills* of the Christian life. The OptIN method breaks out the different spiritual disciplines, sets the objective in each discipline, and then walks participants through standards to help the group reach the goal.

Keep It Engaging

Mastering new skills can be frustrating. Or daunting. Or embarrassing. OR, it can be fun, challenging, and engaging.

Mastery of a skill involves repetition, because skill development is based on "routine expertise."[59] But with repetition comes the danger of boredom. Successful coaches understand that skill development has to be fun; if its not, the monotony of doing the same thing over and over will kill any motivation to do what it takes to excel. [60]

This may be why Sunday School programs struggle with attendance and participation. They lean toward monotony because they focus on learning ideas, over and over. As the saying goes, no one graduates from Sunday School. You move from age group to age group until you age out. In the case of OptIN the goal is to master a Christian practice and then enjoy that practice. The monotony challenge is confronted through group learning and walking away with something new you can do. If learning to ski through practice leads to skiing, then there is a payoff – the joy of skiing. If learning to pray is learned through group practice, then the payoff is – the joy of prayer.

The trade school model is well suited for breaking out of a rut. By adding the group dynamic to the learning process, that is, the workshop format, the experience becomes interactive, and group interaction makes

---

[59] Lucas Et. al., 2012, sec. 4
[60] Coyle 2012, pp. 52–53

the experience fun. In many cases in churches, people watch others (pastors and church leaders) demonstrate spiritual disciplines, but they are then left to figure out *how* to do those disciplines on their own. The result is there is no formalized process to practice and improve spiritual disciplines. Each person is trying to figure it out alone; that is not fun.

Additionally, people in church stall out in their Christian growth and development. While the church teaches and models spiritual practices, researchers in practice know that we only grow to the level of expectation. We grow in resposne to stress, so when someone reaches a level of "acceptable performance", they stop developing.[61] Which means, if we want people to grow in worship beyond what our worship service expects, then we need to create opportunities outside of worship that challenge them, expect more, and stress different parts of their spiritual life.

A stale life of faith results in frustration or indifference, both a common response when there is no clear progress or growth. Our response, the OptIN response, was to provide a platform that jolted participants out of a rut by practicing Christian disciplines together in a way that is engaging, even fun. For those stuck in a spiritual rut, this sort of challenge turns the faith back into an adventure.

---

[61] Ericsson 2016, p. 13.

Chapter 7 – Freedom and the Pharisees

The most consistent theological concern raised regarding OptIN is some form of works righteousness. After hearing our pitch and seeing how we center Christian practices, concerned pastors ask us, "How is this different from the Pharisees, telling people what to do so they can be saved?"

Another way this question goes is, "My people are already so busy. This sounds like one more thing to do, and I don't think I can ask that of them." As pastors, we sympathize with both concerns. There are people everywhere who are stretched too thin and circling burnout, trying to hold it all together at home, at work, in their faith, and in their community. Expecting still more from people, or giving the impression that their relationship with God is subject to some sort of performance review, isn't good news. It doesn't feel like gospel.

The reason we continue to pitch our program and persevere with pastors is because responding to these pastoral issues is more complex than not giving people a to-do list. In this chapter, we will take a closer look at the Pharisees to explore the dynamic between their sinful legalism and the grace of the law. Then, we will look at God's creative speaking in Genesis 1 and Exodus 20 to suggest the cost for congregants when churches don't have clear expectations around a Christian way of life.

Before we proceed, let us be clear about a critical distinction that undergirds everything we propose: Christian practices are a means of grace in sanctification, not the ground of our justification. We practice because we are loved, not so that we will be loved.

Consider how adoption works in a healthy family. When a child is adopted, they receive the family name, full inheritance rights, and a permanent place at the table. This adoption is unconditional and irrevocable. Yet that same family has ways of being together—family rules and rhythms that shape their shared life. Rules like "we use kind words," "we don't hit each other," "we tell the truth," and "we help with dishes" aren't tests the child must pass to remain in the family. They already belong. These practices are how the family lives out its love.

The newly adopted child might initially experience these expectations as foreign or difficult. Using kind words might feel unnatural to a child who learned early that harsh words keep you safe. Telling the truth might terrify a child who previously faced punishment for honesty. But these aren't arbitrary rules. They create the environment where everyone flourishes. In this family, everyone gets to be safe. In this family, mistakes don't get you kicked out, so truth-telling becomes possible. In this family, shared work builds shared belonging.

Over time, as the child practices these ways of being, something beautiful happens. The practices that once felt foreign begin to feel like home. The child discovers they're becoming who they were always meant to be—not to earn their place, but because they have one. The family's ways are forming them into the family's likeness, just as any family changes as new members bring new stories and gifts and challenges.

The blood of Christ alone secures our adoption into the household of God. That adoption isn't merely an idea or legal fiction—it's the deepest reality. The practices we advocate help us experience that reality as an embodied truth. They are responses to that adoption, ways of learning to live as the beloved children we already are. They are how the Spirit forms us—individually and communally—more fully into the family likeness, which is the image of Christ. This is not about earning salvation but about living into the salvation we have already received.

The Real Problem with the Pharisees

Our concern is that the church today is so worried about becoming the Pharisees that we've stumbled into the inverse problem. The Pharisees gave their followers lists of practices to follow. If their disciples did these things, then they were being faithful. Jesus critiques the Pharisees because their practices had become disconnected from their hearts. They prayed, but their prayers were showboating. They fasted, and they made sure everyone knew it. Their spiritual practices, which were meant to draw them toward godliness, had been distorted and twisted inward.

But this is only part of Jesus' critique. Just as important, Jesus condemns the Pharisees for failing to help people enter the Kingdom of God—not someday when they die, but here and now. Life with God is always in the present tense with a future fulfillment. The Kingdom of Heaven that Jesus proclaims has "come near" (Matthew 4:17). It's breaking in today. The Pharisees are religious leaders with the responsibility of helping God's people enter into that present reality of life with God.

Instead, Jesus says in Matthew 23:4, "They bind heavy and difficult-to-bear burdens, and they place them on the shoulders of humans, but they, with their finger, don't want to move them." The Greek word for "move" here is kinéō, which means to set in motion or to help carry. The Pharisees won't even use a finger to help bear what they demand others carry. Later in verse 13, Jesus declares, "Woe to you, scribes and Pharisees, hypocrites! For you lock the kingdom of heaven in front of people. For you do not enter, nor do you allow those who are entering to go in."

Notice that Jesus' critique isn't that they give commands. Throughout scripture, God's words, God's story, and God's commands are presented as a gift—as good news, as life itself. The Psalmist declares, "The law of the Lord is perfect, reviving the soul" (Psalm 19:7). In Deuteronomy 30:11-14, Moses insists that God's commandment "is not too hard for you, nor is it far off... the word is very near you. It is in your mouth and in your heart, so that you can do it." The commands, when properly oriented, are a means of grace. They give God's family a God-like shape.

This isn't what's happening with the Pharisees. Their problem is threefold. First, they add commands beyond what God commands. Jesus confronts them in Mark 7:8-9: "You have let go of the commands of God and are holding on to human traditions... You have a fine way of setting aside the commands of God in order to observe your own traditions!" These additions filter and distort the life-giving purpose of God's law, meaning it is no longer aimed at life with God.

Second, they don't help people carry even the legitimate commands. God's commands are not given to individuals to enact alone. They are given to a community that is called to embody them together. As Dietrich Bonhoeffer observed in Life Together, Christian community exists precisely to help bear one another's burdens, to make possible what would be impossible alone. "The Christian, however, must bear the burden of a brother. He must suffer and endure the brother. It is only when he is a burden that another person is really a brother and not merely an object to be manipulated."[62] The Pharisees refuse to be burdened by the people they serve, and so abdicate this fundamental responsibility.

Third, by both their additions and their abandonment of deeper truths, the Pharisees transform commands that were aimed at life with God and

---

[62] Dietrich Bonhoeffer, 1954, p. 100.

life with one another into obstacles that prevent people from entering the Kingdom. What God intended as a pathway becomes, in their hands, a wall.

This pattern fits squarely within historic Christian tradition's understanding of spiritual formation. Augustine tells us that, "The law was given that grace might be sought; grace was given that the law might be fulfilled."[63] Thomas Aquinas, in his Summa Theologica, argues that external acts of religion must be ordered toward internal devotion. "Now the worship of God is twofold: interior and exterior. For since man is composed of soul and body, each of these should be applied to the worship of God, the soul by interior worship, the body by outward worship... Consequently exterior worship is directed to interior worship."[64] Aquinas holds onto Jesus' prioritizing of this interior worship, but insists the exterior worship is a tool for faithful interior worship. John Wesley's emphasis on "means of grace" and "Christian perfection" held together both practice and heart transformation as inseparable aspects of sanctification.

The Eastern Orthodox tradition has perhaps maintained this integration most consistently, understanding theosis (deification) as requiring both ascetic practice and divine grace, both human effort and God's transforming presence. As Maximus the Confessor wrote, "The whole man should become God, deified by the grace of God who became man, remaining wholly man in soul and body by nature, and becoming wholly God in soul and body by grace."[65]

Our contemporary aversion to the Pharisees has led us to create our own version of heavy burdens, though they take a different form. In our haste to avoid being prescriptive, we've created a less visible set of burdens: we expect individuals to generate their own spiritual desire and program and momentum. We tie up heavy burdens of "You should want to pray more" or "When you really know God, you're hungry for Scripture" or "Your life won't be the same once you experience real worship."

Behind these statements is what philosopher Charles Taylor calls the "buffered self"—the modern assumption that individuals are self-sufficient units who should be able to manage their own spiritual development through willpower and correct thinking. But as James K.A.

---

[63] Augustine, 1887.
[64] Thomas Aquinas, 1991, II-II, Q. 81, Art. 7
[65] Maximus the Confessor, 2014. p. 101.

Smith argues in Desiring the Kingdom, we are not primarily thinking beings but desiring beings, and our desires are shaped by practices and liturgies—either the church's or the world's.[66] Our desires are not a choice. Desires get stuck in us, so it is a profoundly human experience to have desires we wish we didn't, or wish we desired something we don't. While we can't decide to change our desires, our decisions can change our desires over time. What we do, what we watch, who we share life with, the stories we tell, the time we do (or don't) spend with God, the time we spend in service, all of these shape us.

In an attention economy where every app, advertisement, and algorithm is engineered to capture focus, we should ask what has come from the church expecting people to manage their own attention toward God. Churches shoulder the responsibility of inspiring change in people's lives. People are left with the burden of maintaining their attention, sustaining desire, managing willpower, and finding the time to make the change. Which burden is heavier?

This is its own form of locking the Kingdom's doors. We inspire people toward a destination but don't take responsibility for walking with them on the path.

Consider how different this is from Jesus' approach. Jesus calls his disciples to *follow* him. To use Bonhoeffer's language, Jesus burdens himself with his disciples. He invites them into his life so they can experience his way without the responsibility of always wanting to, or always understanding. They are invited to participate in something that they couldn't have earned or achieved. This is grace.

When Jesus says in Matthew 11:28-30, "Come to me, all you who are weary and burdened, and I will give you rest. Take my yoke upon you and learn from me, for I am gentle and humble in heart, and you will find rest for your souls. For my yoke is easy and my burden is light," he's not contrasting work with no work. He's contrasting abandonment with accompaniment. The Pharisees say "carry this" and walk away. Jesus says "take my yoke upon you"—a yoke is shared, with Jesus pulling alongside us. The Greek word for "easy" here is chrēstos, which can mean well-fitted or kindly. It's a yoke shaped for the actual human who will wear it, not a one-size-fits-all burden.

---

[66] James K. A. Smith, 2009, p. 25.

In Matthew 23:23, Jesus tells the Pharisees, 'You give a tenth of your spices—mint, dill and cumin. But you have neglected the more important matters of the law—justice, mercy and faithfulness. You should have practiced the latter, without neglecting the former." The Greek word here for "practiced" is poieō, meaning to make or to do. Jesus isn't rejecting practice—he doesn't even reject their tithing of leaves! Instead, Jesus is insisting that practice must be oriented toward its proper end: justice, mercy, and faithfulness, which are themselves practices, not just feelings or beliefs.

Some will object that Jesus' words were addressed to first-century Pharisees under the old covenant, so they are not a model for the post-Pentecost church. Yet Jesus doesn't abolish the law but fulfills it, re-targeting it toward its true purpose: love of God and neighbor. As he states in Matthew 5:17-18, "Do not think that I have come to abolish the Law or the Prophets; I have not come to abolish them but to fulfill them." Paul makes this same move in Romans 13:8-10, showing that love is the fulfillment of the law, and in Galatians 5:14, declaring that the entire law is fulfilled in loving your neighbor as yourself. The practices continue, but now they flow from grace rather than toward earning it, empowered by the Spirit rather than by human effort alone.

The early church fathers understood this integration well. John Chrysostom, commenting on Matthew 23, notes that Jesus "does not forbid them to listen to the Pharisees, but to imitate them... showing that practice and teaching ought to be conjoined."[67] The practices matter, but they must be connected to their purpose and supported by the community.

When we hear "heavy burdens," we must ask ourselves: Is a program like OptIN just another burden added to already overwhelming lives? Because we take this question seriously, we always practice what we ask people to do. We don't just tell people they should pray—we practice the prayers together. We don't just say stories matter—we create safe spaces to tell them. Following the wisdom of Benedict's Rule, which insisted on moderation and adaptation to individual capacity, practices can be adapted for different contexts—single parents can engage differently than retirees, shift workers differently than those with regular schedules, those managing chronic illness or disability differently than those in robust health.

---

[67] John Chrysostom, 1888.

The key is not uniformity but purposeful engagement at whatever level is possible. As Evagrius Ponticus taught in the fourth century, spiritual practices must be fitted to the individual soul, not forced into rigid patterns.[68] A breath prayer during a commute counts. A one-minute examen before bed counts. But without the practices, the reality of the gospel can be believed in only theoretically. When we experience the gospel as part of daily life, we join the disciples along the road with Jesus.

As pastors, Jesus' critique haunts us. Multiple studies over the past decade consistently show that the majority of young adults who grew up in church withdraw from church involvement as adults. How can we explain a reality like that, except to acknowledge that we were converting people, calling them to kingdom life, and then failing to help them enter in? We were creating our own heavy burdens—not of excessive rules but of impossible expectations for self-directed spiritual formation in a world designed to distract. The formation failure is not just about cultural drift —it's about our failure to equip believers with sustainable practices that connect their faith to their daily lives, practices that hold together both the external action and the internal transformation, just as the church has always taught they must be held together.

A Gospel Exploration

Jesus begins his ministry in Matthew with the proclamation, "Repent, for the kingdom of heaven has come near." After calling disciples and healing the sick, Jesus goes up a mountain and teaches what his kingdom looks like. The Sermon on the Mount describes a way of life: making peace, being faithful even in heart, loving enemies, giving generously, praying humbly, fasting quietly, trusting God to provide.

The sermon's conclusion is crucial for church institutions today. Jesus concludes: the gate is small and the road narrow that lead to life; trees can be known by their fruit; most haunting, those who call "Lord, Lord" but don't do the work of the Father are not his followers at all. The sermon concludes:

> "Therefore everyone who hears these words of mine and puts them into practice is like a wise man who built his house on the rock... But

---

[68] "Against the demon of acedia... one must not set a single rule for everyone, but each must consider what is appropriate for him." Evagrius Ponticus, 1970, p. 29.

everyone who hears these words of mine and does not put them into practice is like a foolish man who built his house on sand."

To be clear: Jesus does not say this obedience earns salvation. When Jesus speaks of fruit, he offers it as diagnostic tool, not currency. He insists, however, that it is a valid diagnostic tool for believers to use. The fruit reveals the health of the tree, which is either being made healthy by its connection to good soil and living water, or it's not. Our practices don't earn our access to God, but as embodied creatures are practices are an essential part of how we are connected to God. Without God's grace, the practices don't work. Without an embodied faith, we fail to let God's grace transform our hearts and minds and lives.

The detail Jesus gives us about the foolish man is that he heard Jesus' words but didn't put them into practice. He could be a student of Jesus with the teachings memorized, all the right Sunday School answers, even a Master's degree in Biblical studies. The problem isn't knowledge—it's the absence of practice. Human beings are embodied creatures, so our faith requires our bodies.

Stanley Hauerwas points out, "Nowhere in Scripture do we get a distinction between religious belief and behavior. The Sermon on the Mount is hardly Jesus' 'ethic,' but is part and parcel of his proclamation of the coming kingdom."[69] To believe in Jesus is to do these things. The instructions and commands are what it means to have faith in Jesus as savior and king. Paul makes this same connection in Ephesians 2:8-10: we are saved by grace through faith for good works, which God prepared beforehand for us to walk in. The good works aren't an achievement, they are prepared for us to join in. We join the prayers, we don't achieve. We receive true stories, we don't facbricate them.

Life Shaped by God's Creative Word

In Genesis 1, the world is described as "tohu wa-bohu"—formless and empty, without life. The chaos and desolation are not hospitable. Then God begins to speak. God creates light, separates it from dark, establishes evening and morning. God creates a vault to separate waters, gathers waters so there is dry land. These first three days, God orders unconstructed chaos into something that will promote life. The purpose

---

[69] Hauerwas 2004, p. 104

of this form is revealed as the skies and waters and earth begin to burst with life.

This theme of ordering-toward-flourishing represents creational wisdom, not merely old covenant law. It tracks through scripture. The Ten Commandments are introduced with, "And God spoke all these words, saying…" God again gives order and form so there might be life abundant. Jesus doesn't reject this ordering but shows how he fulfills it—the Sabbath was made for humans, not humans for the Sabbath; love is the fulfillment of the law. God's commands give life an order, rhythm, and routine oriented toward God.

When the Word becomes flesh in John's gospel, the purpose of God's speech is once again so creation might have life. "For God so loved the world that he sent his only Son, so that whoever believes in him shall not perish but have eternal life." This eternal life is the life of God the Father, Son, and Holy Spirit. Through Jesus, that eternal life can live in us.

In Genesis 1, God spoke creation into a shape where life could flourish. God ordered the chaos by arranging the space of creation so that creation itself was shaped toward life. The 10 commandments do something similar. When Jesus teaches about four kinds of soil, it's not merely a diagnostic description. It's an invitation. The church is meant to be good soil, shaped and ordered so that when people join our way of life, they join rhythms and practices and rules that are shaped toward life.

Freedom in Good Constraints

During my (Brian's) sophomore year in college, I spent a semester in York, England. I was in the middle of sustained depression, and the faith that had grounded me through my teenage years had suddenly dried up. I tried to sing the songs and read the Bible and go to church, but I couldn't hear or feel God in the ways I was used to. My heart wasn't in it, and I couldn't make myself feel it.

A half-mile from my dorm was York Minster, a 235-foot-tall Anglican Cathedral. I wandered in as a tourist one morning and found myself accidentally participating in morning prayer. The youngest participant by forty or fifty years, I imitated my neighbor as they pulled out the Book of Common Prayer. An accidental visit became a regular occurrence. I added evening vespers on Fridays, when the choir would sing hymns and Psalms.

I didn't magically stop being depressed. What I found was a practice that didn't depend on my feeling. I wanted to be with God. I didn't know how to be with God. I couldn't achieve it by my own desire. But the church did. I participated in the life of the church, tagged along as the church went to prayer each morning, listened as they sang the promises of scripture. Like the disciples, I began to realize I hadn't really understood what prayer was. In that season when I couldn't find God for myself, I found God there in those pews and cracked yellow pages. My body kept going when my heart didn't want to, and by the grace of God, I found God was still more than enough.

This experience taught me that scripted and spontaneous prayer are like two lungs of the church—we need both to breathe fully. The structure held me when my spontaneity failed, and later, that same structure would launch me into renewed spontaneous communion with God.

Churches should not invite people to believe in Jesus without clarifying that this belief includes a way of life. Neither should churches invite people to believe without embodying a way of life that congregants can join and imitate. This is the church's responsibility. To do otherwise is to call people into a way of life, then step back precisely where they need help to enter that way of life.

What I found during my semester in England was a structure that had been built toward flourishing with God. I didn't create it. I didn't earn it. I didn't even understand it when I started attending. But in inhabiting it, I found myself moving toward life.

Removing all structures and expectations doesn't free believers to have an unmediated relationship with God. Instead, they must now attempt to grow good fruit under the authority of the world—subject to the pressures of work, consumer culture, algorithms that shape our attention, and human limitations. They are learning from the world's liturgies rather than the church's. The mall teaches its own way of life, offering the allure of convenience and endless choice. But while it promises freedom, it forms us into consumers rather than disciples, teaching us to value efficiency over depth, choice over commitment, consumption over communion.

The Church as Trade School

OptIN began in Scottsboro, Alabama, but it doesn't belong to us. As other churches have used the materials, we've learned from their wisdom and experience. A church of Hispanic immigrants took the Building Stories unit and had all 20 stories shared with the entire congregation as a mini-revival. That would never have occurred to us, but seeing what came from it led us to host our own "story slam."

Our Practicing Prayer unit has been used in Guatemalan churches where the assumed way to pray is out loud, all at the same time, for long spans, unscripted. For these groups, the scripts and contemplative tools were strange and challenging. Precisely because they were challenging, they provided a fruitful growing edge. In our congregation, the assumed way to pray is silent, head bowed, and brief. Public prayer where we share and are vulnerable was our fruitful growing edge.

This is why OptIN offers a scaffold, not a script. Local leaders adapt forms to their culture while maintaining the core purposes. We honor multiple streams of Christian tradition—liturgical depth, evangelical passion for Scripture, Pentecostal openness to the Spirit, Anabaptist commitment to community—borrowing strengths from each while allowing local expression.

The Church is meant to be a trade school for Christian formation. It is not the responsibility of any one church to have it all figured out. It is the call of the Church to be living more and more deeply into the Christian way of life together.

Chapter 8 – The Disciples as Practitioners

"What we are supposed to be doing is making or fashioning Christ-like people… Now, unfortunately, somewhere along the way we ended up confusing 'catechesis' with 'catechism.' We then called it 'Christian education', associating it primarily with only one piece of what catechesis is: instruction, the teaching of knowledge and skill."[70]

It is a great comfort that OptIN is one among many efforts to revitalize Christian practices. The John Westerhoff quote above is an attempt to compare the church's historic practice of "catechesis" with contemporary models of Christian education. He says that we've confused "catechesis" with "catechism." A "catechism," is that document or set of teachings that a believer goes through as part of their entry into church. Christian formation became about providing believers with the transmission of important knowledge and beliefs. Sometimes, this would include the proper skills. Once this transmission was complete, the believer was catechized.

In contrast, Westerhoff says the early church took its task as "making or fashioning Christ-like people." It is not enough to transmit to them what they should know. As a community, we are to encourage one another and build each other up (1 Thess. 5:11), judge one another (1 Cor. 5:12), rebuke one another when we sin (Matt. 18:15), even provoke or irritate (Hebrews 10:24) one another into more faithful living.

Willing Faithful Participants

John Mark Comer helps us understand this reality: "We have created a cultural milieu where you can be a Christian but not an apprentice of Jesus. Much preaching of the gospel today does not call people to a life of discipleship. Following Jesus is seen as optional—a post-conversion 'second track' for those who want to go further."[71]

We acknowledge that discipleship is a trajectory, and we welcome beginners wherever they are on that journey. Yet we must also name the telos clearly: apprenticeship to Jesus. There is grace for the struggling and

---

[70] Watson 2012, p. 16
[71] Comer 2024, p. 33

space for the seeking, but the goal remains transformation into Christlikeness.

Belief in Jesus often means agreeing that following Jesus is a good idea, like believing in eating vegetables or exercise. They are good for you, and you believe in them, even if you don't choose to eat those veggies or lace up those tennis shoes. We recognize that for many, the inability to "lace up" comes from real impediments—depression, chronic illness, poverty, disability, overwhelming caregiving responsibilities. This is why OptIN emphasizes tiny habits and micro-practices as on-ramps. A breath prayer is a practice. A silent "Lord, have mercy" during a stressful moment is a practice. Meeting people where they are doesn't mean leaving them there, but it does mean honoring the genuine constraints they face.

Permission to neglect practices, even for those facing real barriers, isn't "mercy" or "grace" any more than permission to skip eating veggies or exercise is "mercy" or "grace." The point of the practices is that they are tied to health. Spiritual practices are tied to our spiritual health, so permission to neglect them is permission to spiritual ill-health. If the church is committed to the spiritual health of its congregants, then the church will find itself obligated to accomodate the barriers facing its congregants.

In the gospels, belief in Jesus is tied to following him. Following is an act of belief. Jesus sees faith in those who walk, or are carried, or cry out to him for healing. The disciples are those whose lives are uprooted for the sake of following after Jesus. Where Jesus goes, they go. What Jesus does, they imitate. Their faith is not contained to their heart, mind, or personal life. Jesus has claimed it all.

The gap between the disciples and the crowds is not a gap in experience or belief about what Jesus can do. The crowds were moved, fed, healed. They recognized Jesus had power and wisdom. They traveled to hear him preach. And yet, they were not disciples. They didn't reorient their life around Jesus. The gap is one of allegiance and trust.

A model of church aimed at helping people experience the power of Jesus to improve their lives, to show God's power and wisdom, to draw people in to hear his words, is a church designed to create *crowds*, not *disciples*. A model of church that takes these crowds and helps them submit their hearts and minds and relationships and lives to the wisdom and truth of Jesus is a church designed to create disciples.

The Architecture of Our Lives

Our lives have an architecture—habits, schedules, instincts, relationships. Often this design emerges accidentally in response to how we grew up and daily demands on our time. I don't decide on the architecture of my life each day any more than I decide on the architecture of my house. I inhabit it, and it shapes what I do.

This architecture doesn't think or consciously believe things. But it does assume certain beliefs. Different life architectures are faithful to different kingdoms. I might believe it's essential to pray every morning because the Spirit equips me for the day ahead. I might also believe I don't have time because I have to get to work early. These competing beliefs reveal themselves in my morning schedule.

For those who feel they have no control over their schedules—hourly workers with variable shifts, caregivers managing medical appointments, parents juggling multiple jobs—we don't pretend the solutions are simple. But even within severe constraints, small practices can be fitted: a commute becomes a prayer chapel, dishwashing becomes a time for gratitude, the moments before sleep become an examen. These aren't lesser practices; they're practices adapted to real life.

If we're not being intentionally formed by Jesus, then we're unintentionally being formed by someone or something else. This is precisely the reality Jesus overturns when he calls his disciples to "follow me." Their life-architecture with its practices, habits, routines, assumptions and beliefs is displaced so they can learn new truths and build new ways of life in response to the good news of Jesus.

Performance as the Heart of Faith

James Fodor and Stanley Hauerwas examine the Christian life through the frame of a dramatic performance. "What is overlooked by both subjective and objective accounts of faith is the sense in which Christian existence is first and foremost an activity—a performance, if you will. If Christian faith is from start to finish a performance, it is so only because Christians worship a God who is pure act, an eternally performing God."[72]

---

[72] Hauerwas 2004, pp. 76-77

Jesus doesn't teach the Word of God. Jesus is the Word of God. The witness of Jesus encapsulates his entire life, including his actions, his words, and his relationships. His life was a performance of faithfully loving God and neighbor. His followers are imitators of Christ, both by their beliefs and by their practice. And it is the Church that has the role of preparing Christ followers. Thus, OptIN is focused on practices of the faith in the context of the Church.

Following this insight is significant for the church's witness today. Fodor and Hauerwas expand:

> "For one thing, understanding Christian existence as a kind of performance helpfully encapsulates the sense in which both the intelligibility and the assessment of faith are of one piece. That is to say, the intelligibility (and hence the persuasiveness) of Christian faith springs not from independently formulated criteria, but from compelling renditions, faithful performances. In George Lindbeck's words, "Reasonableness, in religion and theology, as in other domains, has something of that aesthetic character, that quality of unformalizable skill, which we usually associate with the artist or the linguistically competent. . . . In short, intelligibility comes from skill, not theory, and credibility comes from good performance, not adherence to independently formulated criteria."[73]

The witness of Jesus wasn't compelling because it was draped in "wise and persuasive words." Instead, it was, "A demonstration of the Spirit's power."[74] In perfect submission to the Father and the Spirit, the fully-human Jesus lived a perfect life. Jesus didn't just preach love. In Jesus we see the coming together of God's truth and beauty in a life that was a perfect performance of God's love. We can trust his way of prayer and his relationship with the Father because it powered the life he lived. We can trust his way of fulfilling the story of God in scripture because of the life he lived. What if we dissected the practices of Christ, and presented ideas on how to break them down into manageable steps? What if we made each successive step a little more complex until we reached a high level of skill in that area? This became our challenge when thinking about the different spiritual disciplines seen in the life of Christ.

---

[73] Ibid., p. 78

[74] 1 Corinthians 2:4

Think of what it would be like to be a basketball team that never practices, never learns skills, and plays so poorly there is no joy or reward. What if that is what we are seeing in our churches? It is an aesthetic reaction to the church's—to our—lackluster performance of the faith. What can be generative for the church is the prescriptive power of this diagnosis. Our congregations need to be equipped for living a compelling performance of the faith.

> "Being disciplined in obedience is perhaps the key virtue of a good and faithful performer. This is a skill that can be acquired only in communities that foster an "ecology of hope," what Nicholas Lash calls "schools of stillness, of attentiveness; of courtesy, respect and reverence; academies of contemplativity." Patient listening and attentiveness are skills that are exercised, honed, and refined in Christian community. Moreover, within the life of the church this type of respectful, attentive listening is acquired primarily in liturgy; this is where Christians learn what Rowan Williams calls "repentant attention"—reverence toward one another and receptivity to God."[75]

Realistically, Christian practice has a tall hill to climb. It is incompatible with the current pace of life lived by most congregants and congregations today. Slowing down isn't positive in itself. Slowing down is necessary to attend to the intersection of God's presence and work with particular people in a particular place. Developing skills, as any person on a sports team knows, takes a sacrifice of time and effort. Faith as performance reinforces the emphasis we've placed on practicing skill. Hauerwas and Fodor note, "At the root of every practice is a way of operating that we learn not by having it explained and justified to us, but by simply doing it, or by being trained into it.[76]

Learning new skills of the faith does not create cookie cutter (identical) Christians. Before we can understand the practice or understand what an excellent performance looks like or feels like, we need to be in it. Adaptation and personalization don't come at the beginning of the process. They come along the way. The skills we learn take on our personality, our flavor, our gifts. Orators, dancers, visual artists, writers, all begin with imitation. Through attentive imitation, they find their own

---

[75] Hauerwas 2004, p. 100
[76] Ibid., p. 104

voice and style. "In short, our God is a performing God who has invited us to join in the performance that is God's life."[77]

If we disconnect beliefs from practices, we produce a distorted gospel, as well as a tedious faith. Beliefs without practice are unsatisfying, and practices without supporting beliefs are potentially dangerous. Absent compelling performances of the faith, the truth of the gospel changes. "Believer" comes to mean a theoretical belief that the Bible is true or that Jesus is factually the savior. Without a compelling "demonstration of the Spirit's power," the church's witness comes to depend on precisely the, "wise and persuasive words," that Paul was rejecting. Discipling in this way roots people's faith, not in the "power of God," as Paul does, but instead in the abstracted coherence of the message itself.

As the church participates together in the way of life Jesus gives us— telling God's stories and our stories, ancient prayers and prayers from our heart, praising the same three in one—we find answers to the question of what it means to perform the Faith. It is a temptation to think we don't need the church to answer the question of how we should personally live out the faith. But we don't learn how to live the faith without participating in the church's life from which our faithful performance is discovered. Jesus doesn't give us the option of ain individual faith, only a communal faith made personal. Hauerwas and Fodor expand on this temptation for the church with an argument that applies just as well to individual Christians:

> The church is too often fickle and unsteady in its commitments, unfaithful in its performance, impatient in its actions. We are too often tempted to trust more in our own timing than God's. Consequently, in many of our well-intentioned strategies, our cleverly devised schemes and plans to save time—even and especially in our theological designs —we end up losing time, falling out of step, precisely because we fail to pay sufficient heed to the hard bodily practices that teach us how to dwell in time.[78]

Hauerwas and Foster reference particular Christian practices, but their primary work is applying a new paradigm to the life of faith. The emphasis of practicing the Faith has helped OptIN with the language of guiding God's people into a faithful performance of the faith.

---

[77] Ibid., p. 77

[78] Hauerwas 2004, p. 107

The Missing Piece in Christian Formation

Richard Foster outlines Christian disciplines including meditation, prayer, fasting, study, simplicity, solitude, submission, service, confession, worship, guidance, and celebration. Dallas Willard names similar Christian disciplines. Both made significant contributions in highlighting the need to recover these practices for Protestant churches that had largely abandoned them.

Willard notes that the church fails "to foster those bodily behaviors of faith that would make concrete human existence vitally complete."[79] Foster states, "It is impossible to learn how to meditate from a book. We learn to meditate by meditating." Here, the medium of church life becomes important. We cannot teach meditation through a book. We teach it by making room for people to meditate.

Scripture itself, while full of practices and their importance, shows us these practices narratively and paradigmatically rather than in step-by-step instructions. We see Jesus pray but aren't given a detailed method. We see the early church share possessions but aren't given an implementation guide.

This isn't a criticism of Scripture's sufficiency but a recognition of how Scripture functions. The Bible gives us the what and why; the church community has always been the context for learning the how. Just as Paul could say "imitate me as I imitate Christ," the church provides living examples and practical wisdom for embodying biblical truth.

OptIN translates these narrative patterns into teachable progressions while remaining faithful to their biblical purposes.

As pastors, we realized we were doing a good job of convincing people that the faith is a good idea. But the faith is meant to be performed. It is meant to be embodied. The living water is meant to be drunk, and the bread of life to be eaten. The Psalms and the Lord's Prayer are not first of all meant to be studied. They are meant to be prayed. With this realiziation, we've been shifting our emphasis. A congregation isn't meant to be an audience. They're meant to be on stage, performing the faith as a witness to the world. And by the power of the Spirit, this performance

---

[79] Foster 2018, 26 of 259, Kindle

exceeds itself, pointing beyond the imperfect church toward the God who leads us.

Toward Sustainable Formation

When we talk about practice-based (rather than just belief-based) formation, we're not creating a new legalism. Assessment in OptIN focuses on gentle competency mapping—observable skills developed over time, with testimonies and stories as primary evidence rather than scorecards or points. Can someone share a story of God's presence in their life? Can they pray spontaneously for another person? Can they identify where they need reconciliation and take appropriate steps? These are observable competencies that emerge from practice, not boxes to check.

The sacraments provide the backbone for this formation. Baptism establishes our identity as beloved children, the foundation from which all practices flow. The Eucharist becomes our regular reconciliation practicum, where we practice receiving grace and extending peace. These aren't additional practices but the anchoring practices that give meaning and context to all others.

Critically, sustainable formation must include sabbath and rest as core practices, not afterthoughts. In a culture of exhaustion, rest becomes a radical act of trust, a declaration that our value doesn't come from our productivity. OptIN units are designed in six-week cycles with built-in breaks, honoring the human need for rhythm and rest. We're not adding to the church calendar but suggesting strategic swaps—replacing low-impact programs with formational units, integrating practices into existing small groups rather than creating new time demands.

The implications extend beyond individual formation. When a congregation practices reconciliation, shares meals across difference, and engages in public acts of mercy, they create a visible plausibility structure for the gospel. The watching world sees a community that actually embodies the peace and justice it proclaims. This isn't performance as show but performance as demonstration—making the kingdom tangible in ways that words alone never could.

If we become formation-focused, our performance improves as we grow in faith. The church maintains one witness, pointing always to Jesus, keeping one scripture. But the language of scripture and the way of life need to be translated into particular contexts for faithful and authentic performance. We practice because we are loved, not so that we will be loved. And in practicing together, we discover that love taking deeper root in our daily, embodied lives.

Chapter 9 – The Fruit of Spiritual Practices

Those who delve into the world of Christian practices give lists of what they are. In the case of OptIN, we started with three areas of Christian practice: Building Stories, Practicing Prayer, and Rehearsing Worship. In addition to these core units, new units have been added to address specific needs (units like: Being Church, a unit that helps congregants understand what it means to be a part of a church; Exercising Leadership, a unit to equip church leaders.) But we are aware that these are not "The List" of spiritual disciplines; they are just a list.

While the list of Christian practices is extensive, what holds them all together is the idea that being a Christian involves practices. Being a Christian is necessarily expressed in what we do. Understanding what a Christian is, and the God Christians worship, also depends on us entering into the way of life that Christians are given.

But the 'doing' of Christian practices is not a form of legalism; we do things because they are beneficial—but more than that, because they are gifts given to us by God through the Church. Grace does not simply change our feelings about what we ought to do. Grace opens a reality we could never enter on our own—heart, body, mind, and soul. It draws us into a shared life with God and with one another. The broccoli metaphor helps here: it is one thing to be forced to eat broccoli when you hate it. It is another to have someone prepare it well, to eat it in community, and to receive it as nourishment. In the same way, when the Church supports Christian practices in the lives of believers, it is acting as a means of grace—a divine gift that makes possible what would otherwise remain beyond human willpower.

Freedom to Practice - Grace

The German pastor and theologian Dietrich Bonhoeffer made the phrase "cheap grace" famous in the 1940s.[80] Imprisoned and executed for his opposition to Nazi Germany, he warned against a Christianity that had become abstract and disembodied—a theology that proclaimed grace while divorcing it from obedience. "Cheap grace," he wrote, "is forgiveness without requiring repentance, baptism without church discipline, Communion without confession, grace without discipleship,

---

[80] Bonhoeffer, Detrick., chap. 3

grace without the cross, grace without Jesus Christ, living and incarnate."[81] Bonhoeffer's warning still stands: the Church's proclamation of grace must always lead us deeper into the life of Christ. That life is neither automatic nor individual. It is something we are drawn into through the community that carries Christ's presence—the Church.

When the Church teaches, corrects, prays, forgives, and gathers us to the Table, it does not do so to burden us, but to sustain us when our own strength, desire, and imagination fail. Because we harbor desires both for God and for the world, the Church becomes the concrete expression of grace that holds us fast to Christ when we cannot hold ourselves. Even beyond our own life and will, the Church continues to carry our story—telling it truthfully in light of Christ's resurrection.

In Growing in the Life of Faith, Craig Dykstra notes that many people perceive Christian practices as oppressive because they "squelch individual freedom."[82] But in reality, practices, when received as grace, teach us what freedom is. "Increasingly," he writes, "we come to live into them until they live in us."[83] Grace does not merely change our desires; it reorients our entire being so that we can live within the practices that sustain communion with God. Someone who runs regularly becomes a runner; someone who prays regularly becomes prayerful. The Church is where these habits are given shape, guarded from distortion, and made durable across a lifetime.

Grace does not replace works—it restores them. Grace is not God's permission to remain unchanged but God's power to draw us into Christ's life. As Paul wrote, "By no means! How can we who died to sin still live in it?" (Rom. 6:2). Grace is God's ongoing action that enables both faith and obedience. Through the Church's sacraments, worship, and disciplines, we are not only reminded of grace but formed by it. Grace is not merely a message to believe but a power that acts in and through the Church's life to make us holy.

This is the classic understanding found in Augustine, Aquinas, Calvin, Luther, and Wesley alike. Grace is not simply divine favor; it is divine participation—the Holy Spirit drawing us into Christ's life so that we may share in his holiness. As Augustine taught, even our willing is already a

---

[81] Ibid.
[82] Dykstra 2005, p. 7
[83] Ibid., p. 45

gift of grace: "God works in us so that we will what He wills." The Church is where that divine work becomes visible and reliable—where baptism, confession, forgiveness, and table fellowship make grace tangible.

In Lynndon Thomas's book on grace he explains the classic Augustinian idea of grace, stating "The saved are free to worship, pray, read scripture, serve others, be humble, show kindness, and be peacemakers. This means that the way to right living involves new desires that are experienced as freedom. Those desires motivate us to righteous acts and attitudes, allowing us to form a relationship with God and others."[84]

Thomas refers to God's expectations as the "to-do list". The practices of our faith, which are on the to-do list, join us with God and others. Thus, the Church's "to-do list" is not a checklist of moral effort but a pattern of shared life that God empowers. Consistent with Augustine's understanding of grace, Thomas states, "we can do nothing without God working in us so that we will want what God wills."[85] The Westminster Confession of Faith makes the following statement, citing Philippians 2:13, "When God converts a sinner, and translates him into the state of grace, He frees him from his natural bondage under sin; and, by His grace alone, enables him freely to will and to do that which is spiritually good."[86] Paul said in Philippians 2:13 "for it is God who works in you, both to will and to work for his good pleasure." The Church, as the Body of Christ, is the very field where this divine work bears fruit.

Richard Foster reminds us that the disciplines are not ways of earning God's favor but ways of cooperating with the grace already given. Dallas Willard says that the disciplines are "actions within our power that open us to a power beyond our power."[87] Grace, for Foster, is Augustinian grace, "God then steps into our actions and, over time and experience, produces in us the formation of heart and mind and soul for which we long. Again, the results are all of grace."[88] When Dallas Willard talks about grace and spiritual practices, he explains that the practices are

---

[84] Ibid., p. 27
[85] Ibid., p. 31
[86] *Westminster Confession of Faith* 1647, chaps. 9, IV
[87] Foster 2018, p. 9 of 259, Kindle
[88] Foster 2018, p. XV of 259, Kindle

done "in cooperation with grace, to raise the level of our lives toward godliness."[89]

The Church's role is to keep us within that current of grace—to provide rhythms, authorities, and communities that hold us steady when our personal willpower runs out. To attempt discipleship apart from the Church is to expect transformation without the tools or structures through which God has promised to give it.

Therefore, grace-driven Christian practices are not legalism. They are participation in Christ's life through his Body. They are experienced as acts of freedom because grace enables our freedom—freedom from sin's tyranny and from the loneliness of self-reliance. As John Wesley described, prevenient grace awakens us, saving grace justifies us, and sanctifying grace perfects us in love.[90] Each of these operates through the life of the Church, the means of grace that Christ himself instituted for our good. They are not mandates; they are an expression of our God-given appetite for what is good.

The Fruit of Spiritual Practices

When grace is received through the practices of the Church, it produces fruit—not only personal peace and joy, but communities marked by belonging and love. Foster said, "The purpose of the disciplines is liberation from the stifling slavery of self-interest and fear."[91] In the Church, that liberation takes flesh. Those who pray learn to intercede for others. Those who confess learn to forgive. Those who gather at the Table learn to serve the hungry. The fruit of grace is a transformed people, and the soil where that fruit grows is the Church.

And this fruit is crucial for the good of the church. Thomas states, "Virtues take love from an abstract idea to concrete actions, which results in others wanting to be around us."[92] Spiritual disciplines allow us to create a community where we can experience belonging and love. Those who practice prayer will be better equipped to pray for others. Those who know how to listen to others will be better equipped to build stronger friendships. Those who intentionally practice confession and

---

[89] Willard 2014, loc. 69 of 277, Kindle
[90] Thomas 2022, p. 91
[91] Ibid., p. 2 of 259, Kindle
[92] Thomas 2022, pp. 75–76

forgiveness will be better equipped to belong to a community of peace. The spiritual disciplines benefit the community of God's people. And as the community becomes a place for rich connection and support, the community motivates greater participation from individuals in developing deeper Christian practices.[93] The benefit of Christian practices for individuals leads to deeper Christian communities, and then the deeper Christian communities feed back into a greater motivation for individuals to be committed to the practices. This push-pull dynamic is what allows groups, churches, institutions to change around a Christ-centered vision.

Of upmost important to OptIN is the church. We believe the church is Christ's Church, and as such it is the best platform for making disciples of Christ. The church *should be* the place where we learn spiritual disciplines. A church that centers Christian disciplines will create a community of belonging; these practices act as a glue that connect us in loving and meaningful relationships. In Acts 2, the Spirit is poured out on God's people. When the Spirit is poured out, the followers of Christ immediately begin to do things: they devoted themselves to the apostles' teachings, they prayed, they worshiped, they ate together, they practiced hospitality, they gave to those in need, and they laid hands on the sick and tormented.[94] In other words, they began to practice the faith. These practices led to a profound community that drew the attention of outsiders: "They were praising God and having favor with all the people. And the Lord added to their number day by day those who were being saved." (Acts 2:47). When the early church, driven by the Spirit, centered the Christian practices, it began to grow, to flourish, to thrive.

OptIN hopes that grace-driven practices can continue to create communities of belonging through which the Spirit can work.

Testimonials

At 86 years old, he had spent his entire life in the church. But one Sunday, after listening to others share their OptIN stories, he stopped his pastor with a question.

"I host a monthly bridge club at my house," he said. "Do you think we have ever shared stories with each other, detailing how God has been present and active?"

---

[93] Dykstra 2005, p. 45
[94] Acts 2: 42-47

Before the pastor could answer, he continued: "No. Of course not. That's what makes church different from bridge club."

In one congregation's second OptIN group, masks were still required and chairs spread far apart in the Fellowship Hall. One of the more outspoken participants admitted early on that while she prayed all the time, she was incredibly uncomfortable praying in public.

As the group worked through the Prayer unit, they prayed scripted words out loud together. They discussed what sorts of things could be said in different prayers. They practiced constructing prayers together, then speaking them out loud while everyone kept their eyes open.

By the end of the unit, this same woman volunteered—that's right, volunteered—to pray out loud for the group. It might seem trivial, but to her it was monumental. She had never been equipped to pray aloud, nor had she practiced it in a casual environment. Centering the practice opened a new depth to prayer she had never previously known.

For a long time, Cindy begged her husband to sing in church. Sitting beside him in worship, week after week, she knew he had a gift. She would hear him play his guitar in the evenings at home and nudge him to share that gift with the congregation.

When Cindy told Mark they were going to be part of an OptIN group, he resisted. He went to church, loved his family, worked hard—he was doing what he was supposed to. Cindy gave him no option to opt out, so they attended with two of their teenage children. Mark was skeptical week after week.

Until the group began sharing stories of God's activity in their lives. Person by person, each one shared a testimony. Learning how to build a faith story through practice proved both inspirational and informative. That's when things broke open for Mark.

He realized there was so much more to the Christian life than he had understood, and that through the practices, God pours into us the peace and hope and joy that characterize so many stories in Scripture. His faith deepened. His hunger for the Lord grew.

So when his pastor asked if he would be willing to play and sing in church, he said yes. No convincing necessary. No begging. He didn't hedge or back away. He committed.

One Sunday school class began using the Building Stories unit as a follow up to other material they'd been working on. The space to tell stories personalized their theological reflection.

"It's been impactful for me personally, for my marriage, and for connecting with others at church in a deeper way," she reflected. "Getting to the personal storytelling was really great and really impactful. It was powerful to relive and retell that experience."

The practice didn't just teach skills. It healed old wounds and opened new possibilities.

One pastor shared, "The Building Stories Unit has been phenomenal—truly transformative for our congregation. We had been through a season of division that left some relationships strained and hearts guarded. As we moved through the storytelling exercises, people began naming God's presence in moments of hurt and misunderstanding. I watched people on both sides rebuild family relationships. It was beautiful to see how the practice of listening and sharing allowed healing to take root again."

A family of four—mom, dad, son, and daughter—was asked to test the Story Investigators Kit. Through fourteen game-like activities, this family laughed, spent time together, and began to uncover ways God had been present in their family.

From the parents' perspective: "We have not had that much intentional, no-screen time as a family maybe ever." "I didn't realize my son had unresolved emotions about that—I just figured he was too young to understand." "The kids were so quick to name how God is present that it humbled me to be more attentive to God at work in my life." "It was the most humbling thing I've ever done to share with my own children specific ways I have seen God move in my life."

From the kids' perspective: "We had so much fun as a family!" "I found that God is working EVERYWHERE! We are such good investigators!"

"My mommy and daddy know God, and now I know that they know God."

By centering the Christian practice of storytelling at home, this family found a richness to their faith and their relationship they hadn't seen before.

She was a senior in high school when she attended an annual youth retreat with about 500 students. OptIN presented a unit on "Being Church," where participants practiced interviewing each other, listening well, and naming their gifts to think through how God might use them.

During one activity, she filled in a chart listing her gifts and passions. For over a year, she had been twisted up with anxiety about her future—confused about a career path, unsure where to get involved. This was new for someone who usually knew exactly what she wanted.

Until she began filling out that chart. Public speaking. Tending to others. Leading groups. Youth ministry. Church leadership.

As she looked at what she'd written, she heard God laughing at her. Literally, laughing.

She realized God was calling her into ministry. She thinks she knew that already, but she had been running as hard as she could in any other direction. Through this concrete, practical activity, she saw the path clearly. Instantly, she felt at peace.

Centering the practice opened a door she had been trying to keep closed.

In a Sunday School class for kindergarten through fifth grade, the teacher used the "Band-Aid" activity from the Story Investigators kit. The activity walks a group through sharing stories of outside scars—physical hurts—that each person has.

One by one, each child shared their story: "I fell off my bike and still have a scar on my knee!" "I was cutting a piece of fruit and still have a scar on my thumb."

Once everyone finished sharing their outside hurt, the teacher prompted the class to share about an inside hurt they had—something that doesn't have a physical scar but that has hurt their heart.

The class went silent. Then, one by one, the children began to share. One child shared about her parent" divorce. Another shared about the death of a grandparent. Another talked about moving away from friends. One young boy named that his older cousin died several years ago, and he still misses him.

At the end of class, the teacher guided the children through a modified Prayer Flip Book she had made. One child chose a prayer posture of lifting her eyes to the heavens. One child chose an image of God to study, the image of the Holy Spirit. And then boy who shared about his cousin flipped through the different scripted prayers that were offered, and he picked the "Prayer for when I'm Sad."

He did not look sad; he wasn't acting sad. But the practice of naming his inside hurt uncovered a sadness that was there, and the scripted prayer helped him put words to that sadness.

The teacher reflected, "If we don't center the practices in this way, our children (frankly, our adults, too) don't ever learn to slow down long enough to feel, to name emotions and pray. If we don't center practices in this way, we don't learn how to name our hurts and then take them to the Lord in prayer."

The children in one congregation love the movies *Inside Out* and *Inside Out 2*. So when their teacher opened up the "Feelings Finder" from the Story Investigators Kit during children's programming, the kids immediately made the connection.

"These are like emoji sticks! Or like the characters from *Inside Out!*"

Then the teacher flipped the emotion card over. On the back was a story of a Bible character who also felt that emotion.

They talked through, "Maybe today you are happy like David was happy when he carried the Ark of the Covenant back home," and "Maybe today you are angry like Esau was angry when Jacob stole his birthright."

One of the younger kids looked up, astonished. "You mean emotions are IN THE BIBLE?!" he said. Then with a thick Southern drawl, "Well I'll be. I just thought it was a bunch of words for old people."

That congregation teaches the Bible often, including in children's ministry. But focusing on emotions brought something to life in a new way to that boy: the Bible is full of real people who felt real things, just like he does.

One youth Bible study meets every Wednesday night, drawing fifteen to twenty students, primarily middle schoolers. Most come from families not actively involved in local churches, and many have divorced parents.

Over the course of a year, the group completed both the Stories module and the Prayer module. The Stories unit had a significant impact, particularly in fostering empathy. Many of these students had only experienced conflict and disappointment through secular lenses.

The unit helped them learn to listen to one another, understand how to encourage each other, and share their testimonies. The students progressed from not understanding what a Christian testimony is to recognizing their own and learning how to share them. By remembering aspects of each other's stories, they connected Bible study lessons to personal experience, deepening their engagement.

The Prayer module introduced them to prayer as discipline, fostering maturity in how they approached God. Studying the Lord's Prayer was particularly impactful, challenging them to focus on God's actions rather than treating prayer as a personal wish list.

Most striking was how the students began speaking about people in their lives with grace and understanding rather than judgment. Some practiced these principles in their own relationships, navigating youth drama with listening, engaging, and forgiving one another.

A woman in one congregation saw the Prayer Flip Book and told her pastor she had to have it. He gave it to her and thought nothing else of it. He knew she already had a consistent prayer life, and figured the tool would end up on her shelf.

She returned months later and told the pastor that integrating this prayer tool into her daily practice had helped her understand the depth of prayer, especially the sensory aspect of it. Looking at the images, all three different panels of the Flip Book, had helped her see her life and the world differently.

She observes the picture, reads a quote one day, and a prayer another day. "The way the quote or the prayer changes how she sees the image has helped her approach God more authentically," she explained. "I don't panic as much. There is less weight on me to pray well because the book helps."

When a pastor introduced a new way of praying the Lord's Prayer—with long pauses between each phrase—her group was skeptical. But as they moved through it together, something shifted in the room.

"There was a holy hush," the pastor later reflected. "Some had tears in their eyes. You could feel God's presence." Just the Lord's Prayer and silence, but the combination allowed them to notice God's presence.

In one congregation, first-generation Japanese Christians shared their stories with the wider church. Many had been kicked out of their homes when they chose to follow Jesus. Some had lost contact with their families entirely.

The pastor reflected afterward: "It's vital for our community to hear and honor these stories. We cannot understand the cost of discipleship for some of our members unless we create space to listen. The Stories Unit made that space possible."

One pastor had a stoic member of his church walk out of a Build Stories class session. The pastor excused himself and followed the man into the hallway, where he found him distraught, in tears. The story prompts had triggered something in the man's past he hadn't been expecting, and hadn't even realized was still affecting him. What followed was a brief conversation and a follow-up meeting. "The focus on stories created a moment for real pastoral care that wouldn't have happened otherwise."

One teenager in a Practicing Prayer group began asking for prayer for his friend. As he spoke, he began crying. It was in the intentional space this group created that he told his parents how his best friend was being bullied and he wasn't sure how to help.

The group prayed for him and his friend. His parents, hearing about this for the first time, were able to support him as he ministered to his friends. The practice of praying together had created a safe space where this young person could bring his deepest concerns—not just to God, but to his community.

A first-time participant in an OptIN group told the story of her OCD diagnosis when she was young and the impact it had on her life. She told about the hope she'd found in treatment and testified to the impact of her husband.

In hearing this story, another member of the group heard their symptoms described. For the first time in a while, they had hope things could improve. After the group ended, this person spoke with their parents and has since received an official diagnosis and begun treatment.

One week later, this younger participant came up to the woman who had shared and said, "Last week, you could have been telling my story. It made me feel like somebody knew me, like I wasn't alone. Thank you."

One gentleman in an OptIN group took his faith very seriously. Yet when it came time to share his story, he told the group that while he knew God had always been faithful to him, he didn't feel like he really had a story.

What followed was remarkable. Several other members of the group briefly shared with him stories of how his faithfulness had made a difference for them—moments when his steadiness had carried them, times when his example had encouraged them, ways his presence had blessed the church.

The stoic and reserved gentleman was shocked and humbled. He was moved to tears. Sometimes we cannot see the story God is writing through us until others tell it back to us.

A new member joined one congregation and immediately participated in a Building Stories group. Sharing stories and receiving them created connection in ways that typical new member processes never could.

"This sharing and receiving of stories helped integrate him into the congregation so well," the pastor reflected. "He felt known and welcomed in a way that went deeper than surface-level hospitality."

Another pastor observed the same pattern playing out across multiple groups: "So many times I hear, 'I've gone to church with you for 20 years and never knew that.'"

Twenty years. Same building, same pews, same potlucks—and strangers.

One participant put it this way after a Building Stories unit: "I've known many of you for a long time. But I feel more connected to you now, although I've known many of you for years, because of our time together. I've been in a lot of meetings and women's groups, mission trips with you. But these stories really do change your lives."

In one congregation, an OptIN group reflected together at the end of the Building Stories unit.

"I do not want it to end," one person said.

"I feel the same way," another agreed. "I was worried about the time, the time to do this, but the community that we built is… Oh my gosh. I needed it and I enjoyed it and I learned things about people here that I thought I knew pretty well."

"I agree," a third added. "I came home every week saying wow, I just didn't know. These amazing people among us, the stories—I mean they were really incredible."

The feedback from pastors running Building Stories groups has become strikingly consistent: congregants who have attended church together for decades are saying, "I never knew that about you."

At this point, this response is so common it's expected—which means it's revealing something at a deeper level. This isn't just a story about individuals learning new things. It's a story about proximity without intimacy, about being together without truly knowing one another.

This is a major story of congregational life in America today. Our neglect of Christian practices has left us with a shallow experience of the gospel.

Arguably, not a single one of these stories is all that incredible. What is incredible is that all of these stories belong to regular churches, with regular pastors. And these aren't all the stories. If all of a sudden, in a church, you have a majority of that church sharing their testimonies with each other and praying in deeper ways and worshipping with intention, what begins to happen is a shift in culture.

There's a lot we're still learning. But here's something we know.

Something changed at Scottsboro CPC **because** the people of Scottsboro CPC changed.

Something deepened at Scottsboro CPC **because** the people of Scottsboro CPC deepened their Christian practices.

Something changes wherever deeper Christian practices allow believers to participate more fully in the life of God and the life of the church.

What we have found is that as more and more people at SCPC have centered Christian practices in their lives, the leadership at Scottsboro is stronger, the volunteers are more abundant, those who make decisions seek wisdom from God before they turn to making a good 'business' decision. The more we center Christian practices as something we do *at church,* we have found: worship is richer, leadership decisions are spiritually grounded, our mission is clear, and our service of others is more intentional.

The fruit of Christian practices is not immediate. But over time, and over a prolonged commitment, the fruit grows. OptIN isn't inventing something new. It's recovering something we've lost: the practice of bearing witness to God's work in ordinary life, and the practice of listening to one another with full attention.

These practices change everything. One story at a time.

The Limits of OptIN

OptIN groups have been formed in over 25 churches in three different countries (the USA, Colombia, and Guatemala). All have had varying degrees of 'success.'

By success, we mean:
- Have individuals developed specific skills in the realm of spiritual practices that support a deeper engagement with the practices?
- Have individuals found ways to incorproate spiritual disciplines into their daily lives?
- Has this deepening of Christian practice among congregants fed into the overall system of that church?

All of our OptIN groups have reported positive experiences with the program. In all of them, individuals have developed new skills that they didn't have before. In all of them, individuals leave with deepened Christian practices in daily life. Every OptIN group reports a stronger connection with others in the group, a strengthening of Christian fellowship with one another. Though many people grow up going to church together, sharing stories and being vulnerable in prayer and intentionally building bonds in worship, allows people to know each other in ways they never had before.

While all of this is positive, the hardest piece to change is the church system. If a church runs an OptIN group or two, the systemic change is negligible. But a church that incorporates the OptIN methodology more broadly, and over a sustained period, we have seen greater sustained change.

As long as practicing the practices is an "add-on" to the life of congregations, the impact will be limited by consistency. We're excited to see what happens as our newest cohort of congregations is experimenting with incorporating the practices more holistically across their church systems.

Chapter 10: Conclusion

Rev. Dr. Kenda Creasy Dean, professor at Princeton Seminary, has been an asset to our experimentation from our beginning in ministry. She tells a story about the American Blacksmith's Union in 1909. They were suffering a dip in membership, but the union rallied. They invited friends, sought apprentices, and the next year enrollment soared. In 1909 the future for the Blacksmith Union looked GREAT! And yet, within 10 years the blacksmith's trade was nearly dead. Unbeknownst to the Union, industrialization was making the blacksmith's trade redundant, inefficient, and unneeded. Men working with hammers over hot metal was replaced by machines that could stamp out hundreds, even thousands of quality tools and molded iron. The manufacture of cars, ships, trains, skyscrapers required mass production, not blacksmiths.

Dean's analogy is that churches and pastors find themselves in a similar position. Her research reveals that two-thirds of 18-29 year olds—after growing up *in* church—"have withdrawn from church involvement."[95] Behind a number that drastic, one might expect a dramatic rejection of church. Instead, "Most U.S. teenagers thus tend to view religion as a Very Nice Thing," but, "just not the kind of thing worth getting worked up about one way or the other."[96] The shift away from church isn't driven by hostility or a surge of disbelief.

For the American Blacksmith's Union, industrialization didn't wipe out their union because Americans suddenly didn't need tools or transportation. Blacksmiths did not disappear from society because people disliked blacksmiths. The demise of the Union came through a system guaranteeing comparable products at superior prices. People weren't mad at their blacksmith. Blacksmiths were simply forgotten, because they were no longer relevant.

The church is facing the same challenge. The models the church has been using, the things it has been offering, are being offered elsewhere. The esteemed British theologian and missiologist, Leslie Newbigin, explains that the success of modern times has broken societal boundaries and produced unrestrained human freedom. "Each person makes his or her own decisions about what to believe and how to behave." We are free to

---

[95] Smith and Lundquist, 2005, p. 124
[96] Ibid. p. 205.

pick our job, home, company, and spouse as often as we like. He then concludes, "It is natural, in a culture controlled by this kind of experience, for religion also to be a matter of personal choice, unconditioned by any superhuman or supernatural authority."[97]

Without systemic change, many churches will find themselves following the blacksmiths: redundant, irrelevant, and forgotten. Without new approaches to Christian formation everyone is on their own, unrestrained, believing and doing as each sees best in their own eyes.

Modern times and the arrival of the "good life" have given us all options. We don't have to pray for our crops to grow—food appears on the shelves. We don't pray for salvation from diseases, we go to doctors, get diagnosed, and take the corresponding regimen of pills and treatments. The explosion of entertainment in the form of TV, movies, theater, cruises, sports, vacations leaves little time for boredom; where once the world shut down so all could go to church, now the church competes with the entertainment industry for people's attention. Technology, science, and experts of all kinds, have replaced the supernatural. And now, people do not depend on the church for their social network. We experience "family" with yoga classes, bridge groups, sports teams, social media, school activities, and dinner clubs. As these essentials are increasingly market commodities, which we can afford to buy, the church has a shrinking number of niches for action:

- The occasional "BIG" stuff — when medicine runs out, when society collapses, when people die;
- The "spiritual" stuff — alongside yoga and therapy, church offers other options for the soul;
- The "nostalgia" stuff — *"After all, the holidays just aren't the same without a family Christmas Eve service."*

Our pews are empty, or at least emptying, not because people are mad. But because they have gone other places to find what they need, and what they want. Maybe standing on the sideline with other parents during a soccer or baseball game on Sunday is more of a community experience than being in worship or attending Sunday school. The point is not to replicate soccer or baseball in church with church gyms and sports fields. Nor is it to provide a Sunday worship production equal to the entertainment of Hollywood. Nor is it to call a dynamic speaker to make

---

[97] Newbigin 1986, p. 13 of 151, Kindle

us laugh and cry. The church cannot out-compete life's conveniences, or out-entertain Hollywood, or provide more connection than sports teams. We are blacksmiths up against industrial powerhouses.

Which is why the church has to return to the thing only the church can do.

In the Old Testament, after Solomon completed the Temple, there was a dedication service. In that day there were greater temples in Egypt than the one in Jerusalem. As rich and wise as Solomon was, there were richer kings. But there was one thing the Jewish temple had that no one else had: "As soon as Solomon finished his prayer, fire came down from heaven and consumed the burnt offering and the sacrifices, and the glory of the Lord filled the temple. And the priests could not enter the house of the Lord, because the glory of the Lord filled the Lord's house. When all the people of Israel saw the fire come down and the glory of the Lord on the temple, they bowed down with their faces to the ground on the pavement and worshiped and gave thanks to the Lord, saying, 'For he is good, for his steadfast love endures forever'" (2 Chronicles 7: 1-3). The Jewish temple had God's presence and those who were there experienced God.

The church does not have to chase better options for the soul to compete with the fields of science and yoga and clubs; it is on the church that God promises to pour out God's Spirit.

OptIN is primarily working to reclaim the things church has historically done. For good reason, churches have tried to compete with the societal institutions that are winning our families, winning our families' time and commitment. But we are not winning the competition.

Winning is the wrong focus for a church. Transforming lives is the real job description of a church.

The Church has promoted spiritual disciplines from its very beginning, not as a form of worshiping self-discipline, but as an act of humility that empowers the believer. Investing our time in Christian disciplines opens the door for God's transformative and sanctifying grace. It is God in us changing us. This was Paul's realization, "But by the grace of God I am what I am, and his grace toward me was not in vain. On the contrary, I worked harder than any of them, though it was not I, but the grace of God that is with me. Whether then it was I or they, so we preach and so you believed."[98] The works Paul did, his accomplishments, were not from self-discipline, thus Paul could NOT brag about all he had done. His works came from God's grace. God was transforming Paul to do things Paul had never done.

Dykstra calls this "habitus" theology, habits which is related to "habitus". Habits are the ways we regularly interact with our environment. Dykstra continues, habitus involves, "profound, life-orienting, identity-shaping participation in the constitutive practices of Christian life."[99] Christians, like all humans, are formed by our habits. The promise of the Christian life, however, is that God's way of life is a way that leads to freedom in God.

The spark that ignited OptIN was the realization that we had people IN our church who were either frustrated with their faith experience or apathetic as a result of their church experience. We had all the right programming: KidsMin, youth, Bible Studies, fellowship events. We had inspiring and faithful preaching. My goodness, we had two young pastors with all the energy (and naivety) to pour into this local church.

The disconnect was something else.

Maybe the frustration and apathy around church wasn't a lack of good doctrine, or good programs, or good people; maybe it was a lack of skills in knowing how to do the faith. It was a lack of habits that shape church identity and participation. It was a lack of tools to help people in faithful experimentation.

Our hope is that churches will reclaim the importance of "putting God's Word into practice," and that by doing so, these churches and the congregants that inhabit them will find they are standing on solid ground.

---

[98] 1 Corinthians 15: 10-11
[99] Murphy, Et. al. 2003, p. 176

Bibliography

Aquinas, Thomas. 1991. *Summa Theologia*. Translated by Timothy S McDermott. Allen, Texas: Christian Classics.

Augustine. 2019. *The Collected Works of St. Augustine*. Edited by Philip Schaff. Kindle. Omaha, Neb.: Patristic Publishing.

Augustine. 1887. *On the Spirit and the Letter*, 19.34, in Nicene and Post-Nicene Fathers, First Series, Vol. 5, ed. Philip Schaff. Buffalo, NY: *Christian Literature Publishing Co.*

Bonhoeffer, Dietrich. *1954*. Life Together, trans. John W. Doberstein. New York: Harper & Row.

Bonhoeffer, Dietrich. 1995. *The Cost of Discipleship*. 1st Touchstone ed. New York: Touchstone.

Chrysostom, John. 1888. *Homilies on Matthew,* Homily 72.2, in Nicene and Post-Nicene Fathers, First Series, Vol. 10, ed. Philip Schaff. Buffalo, NY: Christian Literature Publishing Co..

Comer, John Mark. 2024. *Practicing the Way: Be with Jesus. Become like him. Do as he did*. Random House Publishing Group. Kindle Edition.

Coyle, Daniel. 2012. *The Little Book of Talent: 52 Tips for Improving Skills*. New York, NY: Bantam Books.

Dean, Kenda Creasy. 2010. *Almost Christian: What the Faith of Our Teenagers Is Telling the American Church*. Oxford: Oxford University Press.

Dean, Kenda Creasy. 2016. "Love Made Me an Inventor," Princeton Lectures on Youth, Church and Culture, Princeton Theological Seminary.

Dykstra, Craig R. 2005. *Growing in The Life of Faith: Education and Christian Practices*. 2nd ed. Louisville, Ky.: Westminster John Knox Press.

Ericsson, Anders. 2016. *Peak: Secrets from the New Science of Expertise*. Grand Haven, Michigan: Audible Studios on Brilliance Audio.

Fogg, BJ. 2021. *Tiny Habits: The Small Changes That Change Everything*. Harvest; 1st edition.

Foster, Richard J. 2018. *Celebration of Discipline*. Special anniversary edition. New York: HarperOne.

Hauerwas, Stanley. 2004. Performing the Faith: Bonhoeffer and the Practice of Nonviolence. Baker Publishing Group. Kindle Edition.

Hauerwas, Stanley, and Willimon,, Williams. 1996. *Lord, Teach Us: The Lord's Prayer & the Christian Life*. Nashville: Abingdon Press.

Hiebert, Paul G, R. Daniel Shaw, and Tite Tiénou. 2000. *Understanding Folk Religion: A Christian Response to Popular Beliefs and Practices*. Kindle edition. Grand Rapids: Baker Academic.

Lucas, Bill, Ellen Spencer, and Guy Claxton. 2012. *How to Teach Vocational Education: A Theory of Vocational Pedagogy*. London: City and Guilds of London Institute.

Meadows, Donella H., and Diana Wright. 2008. *Thinking in Systems: A Primer*. White River Junction, Vt: Chelsea Green Pub.

Miller, Lisa. 2015. *The Spiritual Child, the New Science of Parenting for Health and Lifelong Thriving*, New York: Picador.

Murphy, Nancey C., Brad J. Kallenberg, and Mark Nation, eds. 2003. *Virtues & Practices in The Christian Tradition: Christian Ethics After MacIntyre*. Notre Dame, Ind: University of Notre Dame Press.

Newbigin, Lesslie. 1986. *Foolishness to The Greeks: The Gospel and Western Culture*. Kindle. Grand Rapids, Michigan: William B. Eerdmans Publishing Company.

Nye, Rebecca. 2009. *Children's Spirituality: What it is and Why it Matters*. London: Church House Publishing.

Peterson, Eugene. 2019. *A Long Obedience in the Same Direction: Discipleship in an Instant Society*. Intervarsity Press, Kindle.

Plato. 2023. *The Republic*. Kindle. Global Publishers.

Ponticus, Evagrius. 1970. *The Praktikos,* trans. John Eudes Bamberger. Kalamazoo, MI: Cistercian Publications.

Smith, Christian. 2009. *Moral, Believing Animal: Human Personhood and Culture*. Oxford University Press.

Smith, Christian, and Melinda Lundquist Denton. 2005. *Soul Searching: The Religious and Spiritual Lives of American Teenagers*. New York: Oxford University Press.

Smith, Christian, and Amy Adamczyk. 2021. *Handing down the Faith: How Parents Pass Their Religion on to the next Generation*. "Why Are Parents the Crucial Players?" Oxford: Oxford University Press.

Suttle, Tim. 2014. *Shrink: Faithful Ministry in a Church-Growth Culture,* Nashville, Zondervan.

Tanck, Brian, and Micaiah Tanck. 2024. *Building Stories, Leader's Book*. 2nd ed. Scottsboro, Ala: OptIN Publishing.

Thomas, Lynndon. 2022. *Grace, The Desire and Ability to Change, or I Want to Dance*. 1st ed. Memphis, TN: Cumberland Presbyterian Center.

Tilley, Terrence W. 1990. *Story Theology*. Collegeville, Minn: Liturgical Press.

Watson, Paul. 2012. 'Making Christians: An Interview with John Westerhoff', Leaven, Vol 4, iss 3, Article 6.

Westminster Confession of Faith. 1647. PDF digital. https://www.opc.org/documents/CFLayout.pdf.

Willard, Dallas. 2014. *The Spirit of The Disciplines*. Place of publication not identified: HarperCollins e-Books.

Winner, Lauren. *The Dangers of Christian Practice: On Wayward Gifts, Characteristic Damage, and Sin.* 2018, Yale University Press.

Wright, NT and Michael Bird. 2019. *The New Testament in Its World*, Nashville, Zondervan.

Yong, Amos. 2020. *Renewing the Church by the Spirit: Theological Education after Pentecost.* Theological Education between the Times. Grand Rapids, Michigan: William B. Eerdmans Publishing Company.

OptIN has developed a number of tools to support congregants and congregations in deepening their practices of faith. You can explore our resources at optINts.com. Here's a list of our current products.

Building Stories	Participants rediscover their story, notice where God has been moving, and bring it all together by sharing a story from their life with the group.	
Practicing Prayer	Participants intentionally practice aspects of prayer, test prayer tools, then use what they find to design a daily prayer routine.	
Prayer Flip Book	As human beings, we have hearts, bodies, minds, and souls. The Prayer Flip Book helps us draw each part of us deeper into prayer, helping people step out of a prayer rut or stale routine.	
Practicing Prayer: Exercise Book	A collection of the prayer practices from the Practicing Prayer unit, as well as others, to allow participants to continue pursuing new depth in their life of prayer after the unit ends.	
Rehearsing Worship	Participants prepare for worship by building a foundation for why they worship God, and rehearsing what we do in response.	

Rehearsing Worship: Personal Worship Cards	These activity cards each walk participants through a worship service shaped by a particular situation—together, in nature, etc.. These guides are intended as a supplement for the Rehearsing Worship unit.	
Being the Church	This unit helps participants connect their story and their prayers to their church, as they learn to participate more deeply in congregational life.	
Being the Church: Student Cards	These booklets support the Being Church unit, guiding participants as they tell stories, practice prayer, prepare for worship, and build connections within the church.	
Story Investigator Box	The Story investigator Kit helps families investigate their stories and God's story through a series of small, fun, experiments. It helps families connect, with God at the center.	
Exercising Leadership Cards	These cards involve a variety of activities to help church leaders understand their call and practice living into it.	

www.ingramcontent.com/pod-product-compliance
Lightning Source LLC
Chambersburg PA
CBHW060200050426
42446CB00013B/2915